WINNING TENNIS FOR GIRLS

DAVID PORTER

Foreword by
JULIE GREENWOOD

Women's Tennis Coach, Williams College,
2001 and 2002 NCAA Division III Champions

Facts On File, Inc.

WINNING TENNIS FOR GIRLS

Facts On File, Inc.
132 West 31st Street
New York NY 10001

Library of Congress Cataloging-in-Publication Data

Porter, David, 1960–
    Winning tennis for girls / David Porter ; foreword by Julie Greenwood.
        p. cm.
    Includes bibliographical references and index.
    ISBN 0-8160-4814-2
    1. Tennis for girls. I. Title.
    GV1001.4.G57   P67 2003
    796.342'082—dc212002073714

Facts On File books are available at special discounts when purchased in bulk quantities for businesses, associations, institutions, or sales promotions. Please call our Special Sales Department in New York at (212) 967-8800 or (800) 322-8755.

You can find Facts On File on the World Wide Web at
http://www.factsonfile.com

Text design by Erika K. Arroyo
Cover design by Nora Wertz

Printed in the United States of America

VB FOF 10 9 8 7 6 5 4 3 2 1

This book is printed on acid-free paper.

CONTENTS

FOREWORD

One of the beauties of tennis is that, contrary to popular myth, you do not have to be born clutching a tennis racket to play at a high level. One simply needs to learn the basics to enjoy playing a sport that will provide lifelong enjoyment. For the beginner or the accomplished player, *Winning Tennis for Girls* provides a framework for players to build on as they learn this challenging game.

Playing winning tennis requires a single-minded dedication, but it should never become monotonous. As a youth, I found that playing a variety of sports gave me a broader range of experiences to draw from, and generally made me a better competitor. Particularly if you are planning on playing in high school and college, where you will be part of a team, having the experience of competing on a team is really helpful. I most enjoyed playing tennis as part of a team, which probably explains why my best results were in doubles.

As in any other sport, though, individual skills need to be mastered if you want to improve as a tennis player, and this is where coaching comes in. One of the biggest mistakes I see coaches make with young players is that they try and make the kids into the same player. I remember I was a good volleyer, and for a while, one of my coaches wanted me to switch to a one-handed backhand volley, which almost all pros teach. But it was something I just never felt comfortable with, and so she encouraged me to go back to a two-hander. A coach should work with you and help you develop your game in a way that is comfortable for you.

It is equally important that you develop your own style of play that gives you the best chance of winning. This has to do with developing your own identity on the court. Anytime you are playing a match, you need to be able to step onto the court with a sense of how you ideally want to set up the points, and the strengths that you will have against any opponent. If you go out there without those things, it is easy to get lost and just start hitting balls without any purpose. The section in this book on strategies for singles and doubles addresses this in detail, particularly the point that tennis is not just about hitting the ball hard;

you need to think on the court and be willing to mix up how you play, depending on the situation. As a coach, I work with my players on the mental and competitive aspects of their games as much as, if not more than, the technical aspects.

If I were to give advice to a young player, I would say the following: one, you will only improve by playing in actual competition against players who are as good as you or better. Two, try to strike a balance between competing and working to improve the technical aspects of your game. Instead of continuing to work on your forehand, some- times you just need to be in a match where your forehand does not feel great, and play your way through it. Plan your training. Look at your calendar, and look at when you want to be competing at your best. During that time, really focus on match play and not on stroke pro- duction.

Three, spend some time focusing on where your game is right now and where you want it to go. Have technical goals, have competitive goals, and talk these through with your coach. This helps you develop a sense of yourself as a player. Four, try to learn as much from your losses as you do from your wins. As a coach, I've learned a lot from some of our worst losses, as well as from some of our not-so-good wins. Never pass up the opportunity to add to your knowledge of your- self and your game.

Use the information contained in *Winning Tennis for Girls* as you develop your own style and strategies, and you will be taking the first step toward playing winning tennis.

—Julie Greenwood
Women's Tennis Coach, Williams College
2001 and 2002 NCAA Division III Champions

ACKNOWLEDGMENTS AND CREDITS

Special thanks for assisting with the photographs taken for this book to Albert Paulsson, coach of West Windsor–Plainsboro High School varsity girls tennis team, and his talented players: Mahati Acharya, Loren Cheatham, Valerie Chen, and Victoria Sung.

Photographs are by John J. Monteleone, and diagrams are by Corinne Ovadia of Asterick, Inc., Floyd, Virginia.

INTRODUCTION

Professional tennis players like Martina Hingis, Venus Williams, and Lindsay Davenport are some of the most recognizable—and richest—athletes on the planet. But tennis is a sport that can provide fulfillment and lifelong enjoyment for players at all levels, amateur or professional. *Winning Tennis for Girls* focuses on developing the skills needed to play tennis competitively, skills which can be used just as successfully by players who want to turn pro, as by those who only want to learn how to play a sport that they can play well into middle age.

According to recent estimates by the Tennis Industry Association, more than 1 million girls aged 12 to 17 play tennis, whether for recreation or in organized competition. It is not hard to figure out why: tennis is a challenging, yet ultimately rewarding sport that tests your mind as well as your body. Unlike team sports, where there is always a teammate to make up for your mistakes or pick you up when you are down, tennis requires you to dig into your own physical and mental resources on every point. If you like being in the spotlight, you will enjoy playing tennis, because once you are on the court, there is nowhere to hide.

One image that unfortunately refuses to die is that tennis is a "country club" sport enjoyed only by the upper class. Venus and Serena Williams offer obvious evidence to the contrary, but so do countless other players on the men's and women's professional tennis tours, who grew up in modest surroundings but made the necessary sacrifices to become the best they could be. Thousands of other players have parlayed their tennis ability into a college scholarship. Public courts exist in almost every town; a decent racket for a beginner can cost as little as $40 or $50, less than one-half the cost of a pair of basketball sneakers. A can of balls costs $3. What could be easier?

Winning Tennis for Girls will help you get more out of playing tennis, whether you are the number-one singles player on your high school team or just learning how to play. The book will help you to increase your understanding of all facets of the game, from forehands and backhands to drop volleys and doubles strategy. It will teach you not only the strokes you need, but also when and how to use them to your best advantage. In addition, *Winning Tennis for Girls* will focus on important topics such as developing a good mental attitude, choosing the right racket, and avoiding injuries.

The sections of the book that cover the basic strokes of tennis—forehand, backhand, serve, volleying—will follow a basic pattern. Each will begin with a description of the stroke, followed by photos that show the correct form. The sections also include different drills that will help you master the particular stroke. In many places, you will be referred to another section or chapter. For example, the chapter that covers the different types of racket grips is referenced in the chapters that describe forehands, backhands, serving, and volleying. In this example, you may find that it is helpful to return to the original chapter to make sure you understand the information about grips and are able to apply it to the different types of strokes.

1
HISTORY AND ORIGINS

Tennis has roots that go back farther than almost any other contemporary sport. Though the exact dates are somewhat murky, it is generally agreed that the French invented the earliest form of tennis, called *jeu de paume* ("game of the palm") sometime in the 12th century. As the name suggests, players used their hands to hit the ball. The first use of rackets is believed to have occurred in the 16th century, with the forerunners of today's rackets appearing around the mid-18th century.

Until the late 19th century, tennis was played indoors, on a court that hardly resembles the ones used today. The surface of the court was usually stone, with walls on all four sides. The net, often just a cord with tassels hung on it, was suspended across the court at a height of five feet on each side and about three feet in the middle. Players were allowed to hit the ball off the walls as well as off the floor. Tennis balls were usually made of leather stuffed with wool or hair.

The modern game of tennis was developed in England in the latter part of the 19th century, basically as an outdoor version of indoor tennis. Lawn tennis was played on grass courts with lines marking the boundaries instead of walls. Balls made of tightly wound rubber were developed to provide more bounce. Lawn tennis was introduced in the United States in the 1870s, and old photographs and grainy film clips from this era depict tennis as a game played by society's upper classes, with the women in long skirts and the men in long pants, and everyone wearing white.

The first woman to captivate the tennis world was Suzanne Lenglen, a Frenchwoman who won Wimbledon and the French Open six times each in the 1920s and was known for her graceful, flowing style. The first American female tennis superstar was Helen Wills Moody, who won 19 Grand Slam singles crowns, including Wimbledon eight times, in the 1920s and 1930s. Her successors included players like Maureen "Little Mo" Connolly, Althea Gibson, Alice Marble, Billie Jean King, and Chris Evert, all the way up to Martina Navratilova, Steffi Graf, and the players of today who thrill fans with their grace and athleticism.

Men's tennis was dominated by English players in the early part of the 20th century, but by the 1920s and 1930s the English were eclipsed by Americans like Bill Tilden, Ellsworth Vines, Fred Perry, Jack Kramer, and Donald Budge, and Frenchmen Rene Lacoste, Jean Borotra, and Henri Cochet. Australia became a major force in the 1950s and 1960s, led by Ken Rosewall, Rod Laver, Roy Emerson, Neale Fraser, and Lew Hoad. The Aussies were supplanted in the 1970s by Americans Stan Smith, Arthur Ashe, Jimmy Connors, and John McEnroe, as well as a blond baseliner named Bjorn Borg who almost singlehandedly started a tennis boom in his native country, Sweden.

Borg, Connors, and the rest benefitted from a revolution that occurred in the tennis world in the late 1960s, when after much conflict and debate, amateur and professional players were allowed to play in the same tournaments. Previously, most of the major events had featured amateur players while professional players were banned. The Open era of tennis began in 1968 and continues to this day. It took far longer for women to receive prize money equivalent to that of their male counterparts. However, as of 2001, men still received more prize money than women at tournaments like Wimbledon.

Tennis has come a long way since its beginnings as a diversion for the ruling class, and today is enjoyed by people from all walks of life. The professional rankings are filled with players from all over the world, with a high number of players concentrated in the former Communist states of Eastern Europe. Advances in racket technology have made the game faster and more exciting, and have made it possible for recreational players to hit the ball at speeds that the professionals of even a few generations ago could not have imagined. For female athletes in particular, tennis offers unprecedented opportunity: well over 10,000 women play tennis competitively each year at colleges and universities across America.

For those players who have the talent and the discipline to make it into the pro ranks, there is a literal gold mine waiting. Since the start of the open era, prize money has risen in leaps and bounds. When Arthur Ashe won the U.S. Open in 1968, his reward was about $6,000. By the 1990s, the men's and women's singles champions were receiving more than 100 times that much.

Before you start planning your victory speech and where to spend your winnings, however, remember that the players who reach the highest rung on the tennis ladder have all spent thousands of hours on the practice courts and have endured lean times, self-doubt, injuries, and the whole gamut of setbacks on their way to the top. It is also worth remembering that professional tennis players are some of the most well-conditioned and mentally tough athletes in the world. They have to be—their sport requires it.

For all the money and adulation bestowed on today's elite tennis players, the game they play has survived virtually unchanged from the late 19th century. The only significant alteration to the rules of tennis was the creation of the tiebreak set in the 1970s, which had the effect of shortening matches that sometimes had a habit of going on for hours and hours. Aside from that, Lindsay Davenport, Jennifer Capriati, or Venus Williams might be able to go back in time to the 1920s and step on the court and feel right at home. This in itself is a testament to the enduring appeal of the sport.

RULES

THE COURT

A tennis court is a rectangle 78 feet long and 36 feet wide, divided in half by a net 3 feet, 6 inches high. Each half of the court is also divided crosswise by the *service line* with the area between the net and service line called the *forecourt* and the area surrounding the *baseline*—the court's back boundary—called the *backcourt*. The forecourt is divided lengthwise into two boxes—the *service courts*. Each service court measures 21 feet from front to back, and 13¹/₂ feet from side to side.

The full width of the court is used when playing doubles. When playing singles, one uses the *singles sidelines*, which make the court 4¹/₂ feet narrower on each side, as boundaries. This 4¹/₂-foot wide strip that runs the length of the court on each side is frequently referred to as the *doubles alley*. Any shot that lands on any part of the sidelines or baseline is in play.

The racket

THE RACKET

Rackets come in all shapes and sizes, but there are some standards all rackets must conform to. For example, the racket

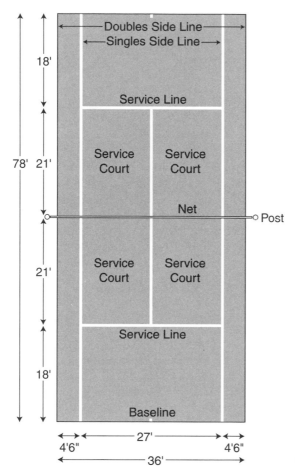

Tennis court dimensions

frame cannot measure more than 29 inches from end to end, or more than 12½ inches in width. The hitting surface of the racket must measure 15½ inches long and 11½ inches wide or smaller. The strings may not have any attached objects except those used to reduce vibration.

PLAY

Before play starts, the choice of ends and server in the first game is decided by a coin toss or by spinning a racket and picking which direction the logo at the base of the handle is pointing. The player who wins the toss may choose either to serve first, or which end of the court she would like to start play.

The ball is put into play by the server, who stands behind the baseline and serves the ball to the receiver on the other side of the net, who customarily stands at the far baseline. The serve must land in the service court to start play. The server gets two chances per point to put her serve in the box; if both serves hit the net or do not land in the box, it is called a fault and the receiver wins the point. Though the receiver is customarily obligated to play to the server's pace, you should not serve until your opponent is ready.

The first point is served into the left service court, or *deuce court*. The next point is served into the right service court, or *ad court*. Each point alternates in this manner until the end of the game. After the first game, the receiver becomes the server, and the players alternate serving one game each. Players change sides (the *changeover*) after each odd game—the first, third, fifth, and so on. This means that if a player wins a set by the score of 6-2, the players remain on the same sides of the court for the first game of the next set, before switching sides.

Players are allowed a maximum of 90 seconds during changeovers, and two minutes between sets.

SCORING

In traditional tennis scoring, the first player to reach four points in a game wins, provided she wins by at least two points. If a player wins the first point, the score is called 15 for that player. The second point is called 30 for that player, and the third point is called 40 for that player. The fourth point is scored as game. The server's score is always announced first; for example, if you are serving and you win the first point but your opponent wins the next two points, you would call out "15-30" before serving the fourth point of the game.

In situations where there is no chair umpire or announcer calling out the score, it is best to say the score out loud before each point when you are serving, to prevent you or your opponent from getting the score wrong and causing a dispute.

If both players have won three points, the score is called deuce, and the next point won by a player is scored advantage, or *ad*, for that player. If the same player wins the next point, she wins the game. If the other player wins the next point, the score goes back to deuce, until one player wins two consecutive points after the score is deuce.

In some situations you may play using what is called a no-ad scoring system. In this format, if the score gets to deuce in a game, the winner of the next point wins the game.

The receiver gets to choose whether she wants to receive the serve in the deuce court or ad court.

Most tennis matches are best two-of-three sets. The first player to win six games wins a set, provided the margin is two or more games. If the score in games reaches 6-6, a 12-point tiebreak usually is played to determine the set winner. In the tiebreak, the first player to reach seven points, with a margin of at least two points, wins the set. The tiebreak set will continue until one player has reached at least seven points with a two-point margin.

Whichever player was due to serve the next game when the set score reaches 6-6 is the first server in the tiebreak. She serves the first point, after which the serves alternate two at a time for each player. The players change ends after every six points.

SERVING

The server must stand behind the baseline and on either side of the center mark, which is a short line perpendicular to the baseline that divides the baseline into two halves. To serve to the deuce court, the server must stand to the right of the center mark. To serve to the ad court, she must stand to the left. Where you choose to stand on either side of the center mark will depend on your serving style, the score, what type of serve you want to hit, and to what location.

Everyone's service motion is slightly different. But all servers must keep their feet from touching the baseline or the center mark from the time they reach a stationary position before they start their service motion, until the time they hit the ball. If either foot touches the base-

Serve position—deuce court (singles)

Serve position—ad court (singles)

Foot-fault—correct positioning

line or center mark, or touches the inside of the court, you will be assessed a foot fault, which is the same thing as if you had served a ball into the net. Once your racket strikes the ball, your momentum can carry you onto the court with no penalty.

A service *let* occurs when the ball touches the top of the net and lands on the receiver's side of the court in the service court. If this is the case, the serve is retaken, with no fault called.

THE BALL IN PLAY

A ball is in play from the moment it is served by the server. Unless a fault or a let is called, it remains in play until the point is decided. A point is ongoing until one of the following happens:

1. The ball bounces twice on one side of the court before the player on that side of the court returns it over the net;

2. The ball hits the ground outside the court boundaries;
3. One of the players hits the ball into the net;
4. A player deliberately hits the ball with her racket more than once;
5. A player touches the net with her racket or any part of her body or clothing, or touches the ground on her opponent's side of the court;
6. A player reaches over the net to volley a ball before it has passed the net;
7. The ball touches one of the players anywhere except on her racket or on her hand or hands that is holding the racket.

COACHING

Unless you are competing in a team-style competition, you are not allowed to receive coaching during a match. This includes having a coach yell things from the bleachers or communicate via hand signals. Breaking this rule can lead to point penalties, or disqualification.

JENNIFER CAPRIATI

Few players in the history of tennis had a more anticipated debut than Jennifer Capriati. Two weeks shy of her 14th birthday when she played her first professional match in 1990, Capriati had already staked her claim as the sport's hottest young property by winning the French Open and U.S. Open junior (18-and-under) titles as a 13-year-old. Over the next 12 months she went on to win her first tour event and became the youngest player to be ranked in the top 10 in the world.

The dizzying ride continued for another two years, but beneath all the hype and hoopla, something was gravely wrong. By 1993, Capriati was barely interested in playing anymore. After an early loss at the 1993 U.S. Open, she dropped off the women's tour and played just one match over the next two and a half years.

Something inside Jennifer Capriati still loved the game of tennis. More important, her personal turmoil had not changed the fact that she still had the heart of a competitor. So, she vowed to return to the pro tour, but this time as a more mature player, one who would appreciate the lows as well as the highs. In 1999, Capriati won her first tournament in more than six years, and in 2001, won the Australian and French Opens and reached the semifinals at Wimbledon. Her career is proof that the journey can be as rewarding as the destination.

3 EQUIPMENT

CHOOSING A RACKET

It would be hard to overemphasize the effect that advancements in racket technology have had on tennis. Each year, new and supposedly improved models are unveiled, with ever-higher price tags. Today's rackets weigh far less than their wood predecessors and can generate so much more power that it almost seems as though today's players are playing a different game than those played in the early 1980s.

All of that is nice; but the question is, what kind of racket is right for you? When the choices range from a $50 model to one that costs close to $500, what's a player to do?

There are some guidelines to follow when you are choosing a racket. If you are a beginner, you should probably start with a basic racket that has an oversized head (see Head size description below) so that you can get used to hitting the ball on the strings with a decreased chance of mishits. For intermediate and advanced players, however, the type of swing you have and the style you play will be factors in choosing the right racket.

As a general rule, if you are a power player—which means you hit the ball with a lot of pace—then you may benefit from using a racket with a smaller head and a normal body, which will give you more control over your shots. If you are more of a finesse player, and particularly if you use a shorter or more compact stroke, you may do well to use a racket with a bigger head and a wide body to provide more power.

There is no substitute, of course, for comparing models. Try out as many as you need until you find the one that suits your style of play, your physical characteristics, and your overall needs (this includes price!). Each racket will feel different, so the right one is out there—you just have to find it.

The following is a breakdown of the different components that make up a tennis racket, and how to make each one fit your needs.

Composition

Today's rackets are made of lightweight materials like graphite, kevlar, and fiberglass. Rackets made solely of graphite tend to be lighter, but also stiffer, while rackets that use a combination of materials tend to be more flexible. If you are a beginner or are still working at mastering the basic strokes, it probably makes sense to get a more flexible racket that will enable you to hit with better control. A stiffer racket, meanwhile, lessens stress on your elbow by absorbing most of the vibration of the ball.

Grip Size

Racket handles are sized in $1/8$th-inch increments. Your grip size will depend chiefly on the size of your hand, but that is not always the sole deciding factor. For instance, some players prefer a smaller grip because it makes them feel like they have better control of the racket. If the grip is too small, however, it may create too much wrist action in your stroke and lead to arm or elbow injuries. Similarly, using a racket with a grip that is too big can force you to grip the racket too tightly to compensate, which can also lead to forearm or elbow problems.

The racket should feel comfortable when you hold it, when you swing it, and when you make contact with the ball. Try a few different sizes before you make your final decision. Remember that you can always put a rubber sleeve or over-grip over the racket handle to widen the grip by about $1/16$th of an inch.

Length

In recent years, racket manufacturers have begun making *long-body* rackets that are as long as tennis rules allow (29 inches). Be forewarned that these rackets can be difficult to get used to, especially if you are accustomed to playing with a shorter racket. As you would imagine, these rackets make it easier to reach balls that are far away from your body, but make playing balls hit into your body more difficult to control. The standard size for most rackets still is in the $27^{1}/_{2}$- to 28-inch range, which is an easier size to handle for smaller players.

Racket Width

The term *wide-body* refers not to the size of the racket head—the hitting surface—but to the width of the racket head. Hold a wide-body racket on its edge next to an old wood racket and you will see that the wide-body head is almost twice as wide. More than any other racket innovation, the wide-body design has brought more power to the game of tennis. The problem is that many beginning or recreational players, in their eagerness to hit the ball harder, end up sacrificing control and spraying shots all over the place. The added power supplied by the wide-body racket means that any flaw in your stroke will be magnified.

If you are a power hitter already, you may want to use a smaller racket that provides more control, whereas if you are a player who relies on finesse, you may want to try a wider racket that will give some power to your groundstrokes. Try out several different kinds of rackets of both types to see which one(s) will give you both the power and control that fit into your game.

Head Size

Oversize rackets, which have a head size of anywhere from 107 to 135 square inches, can make you more consistent by cutting down on mishits, though you may give up some control. Midsize rackets (100 to 106 square inches) give you more control without sacrificing too much power, while traditional rackets (100 square inches and smaller) sacrifice power for more control. Beginning players, particularly if they are short or small, may have difficulty handling an oversize racket and may want to start with a midsize model.

Strings

Most strings are made of synthetic materials like nylon, Kevlar, and titanium, while some are made of natural gut. Natural gut strings generally provide the best feel, but they are not as durable as synthetic strings and will wear out more easily. Synthetic strings are preferable for beginners and recreational players. If you hit with heavy topspin, you may want to use a thicker-gauge string such as 15 gauge, which will last longer than thinner 16- or 17-gauge strings.

String Tension

String tension can vary widely from player to player depending on skill level and style of play, which is why manufacturers recommend tension ranges for all the rackets they produce. Always stay within the limits set by the manufacturer. Stringing your racket at a lower tension, such as 45 pounds, will make the strings more flexible and give you more power, but will also make your shots harder to control. Higher tensions, in the 60s, for example, will provide more control but can make the racket head less flexible and cause your arm to absorb more vibration from the racket. This could lead to elbow problems.

4

GRIPS

There is more than one way to hold a tennis racket; in fact, there are several, and each one can be used to hit different shots and put different spins on the ball. You can ask your coach or instructor which one might be the best for you, but you should try them all to get a feel for yourself. Remember that it is never too late to learn a new racket grip if you want to upgrade your game or learn some new shots.

The handle of a tennis racket is shaped like an octagon, or eight-sided figure. Numbering each side, also called a *bevel*, makes it easy to see where your hand should be positioned on the racket for each grip. The parts of your hand that we will refer to are the base knuckle of your index finger and the heel pad of your palm.

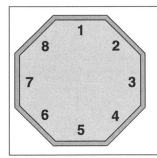

Key:
1. Top bevel
2. Top right bevel
3. Right bevel
4. Bottom right bevel
5. Bottom bevel
6. Bottom left bevel
7. Left bevel
8. Top left bevel

Racket handle bevels

TYPES OF GRIPS

Continental Grip

This is one of the most common grips, and is used by most players when they are volleying. It also is a good grip to use when you want to hit a forehand or backhand slice, or a slice serve.

The Continental grip is sometimes called the hammer grip, because you are holding the racket much in the same way you would hold a hammer. Your base knuckle should be at about bevel 2 (assuming you

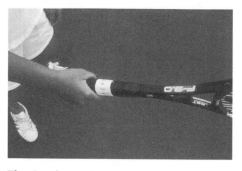

The Continental grip

are right-handed; bevel 8 if you are left-handed), as if you were shaking hands with the racket. Your heel pad should be on bevel 1 or 2.

Holding the racket with a Continental grip, you can see how it is possible to hit either a backhand or forehand volley, or backhand or forehand slice, without changing your hand position.

Eastern Grip

This is a versatile grip that can be used to hit a flat ball or ball with topspin, or a flat, spin, or kick serve. Instructors frequently recommend that beginning players start with an Eastern grip.

For an Eastern forehand grip, if you are right-handed, imagine that you are rotating your hand and wrist slightly to

The Eastern grip

the right, so that your base knuckle is at bevel 3, and your heel pad is at bevel 2 or 3. For an Eastern backhand grip, put your base knuckle at bevel 7 and your heel pad between 7 and 8.

The Semi-Western grip

Semi-Western Grip

The Semi-Western grip is useful if you want to put heavier topspin on your shots. You will sacrifice some power with this grip, but the topspin will cause your shots to bounce higher in your opponent's court and make returns more difficult.

For a Semi-Western forehand grip, rotate your hand even more to the right than the Eastern forehand grip, so that your base knuckle and heel pad are both at about bevel 4. For a Semi-

Western backhand grip, your base knuckle and heel pad should both be about bevel 6.

Western Grip

The Western grip is used mainly by advanced players who want to hit with tremendous topspin, which can be useful when you are playing on a slow surface such as clay. Some professional players use such an exaggerated Western grip that they are able to hit forehands and backhands with the same side of the strings and

The Western grip

without changing their hand position on the racket handle. This is a very difficult method to master, and should be attempted only after you have found a more comfortable, basic grip to use.

For a Western forehand grip, hold the racket with your base knuckle and heel pad both at about bevel 5. This will feel awkward at first, but will become comfortable as you hit more balls.

5 FOOTWORK

Once you have reached a certain skill level and have begun playing in tournaments or for your high school team, you will be facing players who can hit the ball as strongly and as accurately as you can. So, how can you get an edge? Well, one of the reasons players like Martina Hingis and Venus Williams are at the top of the women's tennis rankings has nothing to do with their ability to hit a 120-mph serve or paint the corners with their groundstrokes. Instead, it is footwork and agility that can make the difference between a good player and a great one.

Think about it: it doesn't matter how great your forehand is if you don't use your feet to get in the proper position to hit correctly. For the same reason, if you don't recover from hitting a shot in time to be ready to play your opponent's return, you increase your risk of being out of position and losing the point.

Whether you are a touring pro or just starting to learn how to play, good footwork can improve your strokes, help you hit the ball harder and more accurately, and enable you to return more shots and stay in the point longer. In short, it is the foundation for just about everything you do on the tennis court.

BASIC STANCE

The Ready Position

Next time you are watching a professional tennis match, pay attention to what the players do when they are not in the act of hitting the ball. In other words, how they get themselves ready to return the ball, and how they recover after they have hit the ball. This is called the Ready position, and though it may sound like a simple thing to do, it is surprising how many young players forget to do it or do it incorrectly.

The Ready position is used in other sports besides tennis. A football linebacker will use a similar stance, as will a baseball infielder, although the baseball infielder may lean forward more to get ready to field a ball hit on the ground.

The fundamentals of the Ready position are as follows:

The Ready position

1. Stand with your feet a little more than shoulder width apart, then move them out a little further.
2. Lean forward slightly while keeping your back straight.
3. Bend your knees so that when you lean forward and let your arms dangle in front of you, you can touch the top of your kneecaps while keeping your back straight.
4. Keep your feet firmly on the ground, but transfer most of your weight to the balls of your feet.

You are now in position to react to your opponent's shot. Your lower center of gravity gives you power when you push off with your legs to hit the ball; the wide stance gives you better balance, making it less likely you'll trip over your feet while moving laterally; and your slightly forward-leaning posture is starting you in the right direction to meet the ball.

Ready position, close-up of feet

It may take a little time to get used to this position, and you will probably feel the strain in your leg muscles at first. But if you practice getting in the Ready position before and after each shot, you will eventually find yourself doing it automatically.

The Split Step

Whether you are awaiting your opponent's serve or coming to the net to hit a volley, it is vital that you maintain your balance so that you

The Split step

can hit the ball with power and accuracy. You can accomplish this by using what is called a Split step, which widens your stance and gets you ready to react and move quickly to either side without losing your balance.

The Split step is actually more a small hop than a step. What you are doing is splitting your feet apart about three or four inches farther than they are when you start. The key to the Split step is to time it so that your feet touch down at the moment that your opponent's racket makes contact with the ball. You should land with your knees bent and your body leaning slightly forward, with most of your weight on your toes. This will get you ready to move to the left or right, depending on which side the ball is hit to.

Wait until you can see which side the ball is hit to before you begin to move your feet. Anticipating where the ball is going may work a few times, but when it doesn't, you usually end up hitting a weaker return because you are too out of position to generate much power. You also run the risk of suffering a groin pull or lower back injury if your upper and lower body are moving in different directions at the same time.

Your move to the ball should be fluid and continuous, beginning with your lower body. Start by turning your hips, knees, and ankles in the direction of the ball. As you push off, turn your shoulders in sync with your lower body and lean your shoulder slightly toward the net. For example, if you are right-handed and you are hitting a backhand, you should drop your right shoulder slightly as you move to the ball in anticipation of hitting the shot.

Drill

Stand behind the baseline in the Ready position and pretend your opponent has just hit a shot to your forehand. Do a Split step, take three steps to your right (if you are right-handed), and hit an imaginary forehand. Remember to keep a low center of gravity and drop your left shoulder slightly as you prepare to "hit" the ball. Repeat on the backhand side, then mix it up as if you are playing a point. Next, have someone feed you balls to either side and repeat the drill.

Imaginary forehand: preparation

Imaginary forehand: backswing

Imaginary forehand: contact

MONICA SELES

Most tennis players define adversity in terms of tough losses, slumps, or other routine obstacles. For Monica Seles, the word took on a whole new meaning on May 30, 1993, a day that changed her life forever but failed to blunt her competitive spirit.

It was on that day that a mentally unstable fan stabbed Seles in the back during a changeover in a tournament in Hamburg, Germany. The sight was the most horrific seen at any tennis event before or since: the world's No. 1 player sitting on the clay court, dazed and bleeding from the attack. It would be months before Seles could think about picking up a racket again, and longer before she would even want to. But more than two years after the attack, she returned to the pro tour and remains one of the top players in the game.

To anyone who had watched Seles play over the years, her comeback was hardly unexpected. In a sport where mental toughness frequently separates the contenders from the pretenders, Seles is as tough as they come. She underwent a lengthy rehabilitation to regain her physical strength, but the psychological recovery took longer. If she returned, would she risk being attacked again? Would she be able to play at the level she was accustomed to?

Some of the questions were answered when Seles made her return in 1995. She won her first tournament, then reached the U.S. Open final and lost in a memorable match against Steffi Graf. But, sadly, her struggles were not over; her father, Karolj, Monica's coach and biggest supporter, who used to practice with her in a parking lot when she was a little girl, passed away in the spring of 1998. Again, Seles showed her mental resolve by not only competing in the French Open three weeks later, but advancing all the way to the final before losing to Arantxa Sanchez Vicario.

Today, Monica Seles is still in the top 10, 12 years after reaching that plateau for the first time. After what she has been through, how does she do it?

"It's so simple," she told *Tennis Magazine* in 1999. "I love to play tennis. If someone would have told me when I was 6 years old that all these things would come with it—the money, the fame, the nice people and the things they give you—I would have said, 'That's impossible.' I had no concept of the Grand Slams. For me, it was the pure joy of playing tennis."

6

GROUNDSTROKES

SETTING UP/PREPARATION

Your preparation to hit a groundstroke begins even before your opponent hits the ball back to you. You should be in the Ready position, which is covered in Chapter 5: feet a little more than shoulder width apart, knees slightly bent, upper body leaning slightly forward with your back straight, weight on the balls of your feet and distributed between your thighs, quadriceps, and calves. You are now ready to make an explosive first step to the ball.

Your racket should be in front of you with the head pointing up and out from your body, so that you are in position to start your backswing to make a shot from either side. If you hit with one hand, keep your nonhitting hand lightly around the shaft of the racket just below the head; this will help you move smoothly to either side and keep your racket in a steady position before you begin your backswing.

The next move is to identify (as quickly as possible) which side the ball is coming to, and then rotate your upper body—shoulder, trunk, and hips—accordingly. Many players like to take a small *ready hop* as their opponent prepares to hit the ball, timing their landing to when the ball is struck. This is particularly effective when you are returning serve. The hop essentially makes you weight-

Preparation

less for a split second, and enables you to react quickly when your opponent hits her shot. For a right-handed player hitting a forehand, this means rotating to the right, so that the left, or *lead* shoulder is facing the net.

Simultaneously, bring the racket back with the head facing up and your hand slightly above the level of your hips. This is the beginning of a continuous loop; you will eventually make contact with the ball at the completion of the loop. Your left leg should follow your upper body and pivot forward, so that you are standing almost sideways to the court (there will be situations when you will not have time to make a full rotation, and you will have to hit the ball from an open position in which you are more or less facing the net).

Where you make contact with the ball will depend on what type of grip you are using and what kind of stroke you are hitting. For most strokes, you want to make contact with the ball out in front of you, which means in front of an imaginary line drawn from your lead shoulder and parallel to the baseline.

As you prepare to hit the ball, your weight is transferred from your back foot to your front foot, as your body moves forward into the shot. After you have followed the ball all the way into your racket and made contact, a long follow-through is essential to generate power and accuracy. Since most players shortchange their follow-throughs, practice making what seems like an exaggerated follow-through when you are working on your strokes. It will probably end up being closer to what you should be doing anyway.

Positioning

One mistake that many players make is to not position themselves properly, so that they are moving forward when they hit the ball. This is not always possible, of course; for example, your opponent may have hit a shot that forces you to run laterally or diagonally away from the net to retrieve it.

For shots that are in front of you, however, it is important to prepare correctly to get the most power and consistency on your return. This is most important on balls hit deep into your court. You want to avoid hitting while you are off-balance or moving backward, so you have two basic options: stand farther back—a few steps behind the baseline instead of on the baseline or in front of it—so that you can move toward the ball and not away from it or take the ball *on the rise,* which means hitting it while it is still rising off the ground, before it reaches the top of its arc. The drawback to the first method is that you risk giving up too much of the court to your opponent. The drawback to the second method is that hitting on the rise is a skill that many pros have difficulty mastering.

Since you want to try and hit the ball with as consistent a motion as possible, it is important not to merely move to where the ball is going to hit the ground, but to move to where the ball is going to bounce. This way, you can adjust your stroke so that you hit the ball with a consistent motion each time.

Tip: One way to ensure that you are moving forward on your groundstrokes is to drag your back foot while you are hitting the ball. You may wear out a pair of sneakers more quickly this way, but it will get you in the habit of transferring your weight forward.

Turn, Turn, Turn

There will be many occasions when you won't have time to turn your body to hit a groundstroke. When you are returning a serve, for instance, often you only have time to react and hit a shot from an *open stance*—in which your shoulders are about parallel to the baseline and you are facing the net—instead of having the time to turn to either side to hit your shot.

You can still generate power when hitting out of an open stance, however. One way to practice hitting from this position is to sit in a chair facing the net and hit ground strokes from either side. You will find that you can generate more power than you think.

Getting the Racket Back

Just as there will be occasions when you won't have time to turn your body when you are hitting a groundstroke, there also will be occasions when you won't have time to bring your racket all the way back. This is not necessarily a bad thing; watch some of the top pros return serve, and you will notice that most of them use a shorter, more compact backswing that still enables them to get power on their return.

Though many coaches still preach the advantages of getting your racket back on every shot, the key is not so much having your racket back as it is having your racket in a Ready position, prepared to meet the ball. One way to accomplish this is to bring your racket out to the side first; then, depending on the pace of the shot, you can either take a full backswing or a shorter swing. Either way, you are prepared. It may help to approach it as if you were hitting a volley instead of a groundstroke—racket out to the side, short swing, drive through the ball.

The Follow-Through

The follow-through may be the part of the forehand that is most often overlooked by inexperienced players. It isn't hard to figure out why:

The follow-through

you have already made contact, the ball is on its way over the net (presumably), and you need to prepare for your opponent's return. But an adequate follow-through is essential to generate power and maintain consistency. Cutting short your swing will result in weaker shots and more errors because you are essentially punching at the ball instead of swinging through it. Think of it this way: you are making contact with the ball less than halfway into your swing. That means you still have a big part of your swing to go. Don't shortchange yourself.

In a typical forehand follow-through, your racket arm continues the stroke after contact and goes across your body, finishing up with the racket above your opposite shoulder. The top players often finish their forehands with their racket hand at eye level and the racket head well above their own head.

7

THE FOREHAND

THE BASICS

Getting Ready

As we mentioned in the general section on groundstrokes, your forehand preparation begins with a small hop, often called a ready hop, timed to the moment when your opponent hits the ball. This will prevent you from being caught flat-footed and get your leg muscles ready to react to your opponent's shot. Keep your eyes on your opponent and on the ball; she may be doing something that telegraphs where she is going to hit the ball.

Once you've identified the ball coming to your forehand side, keep your eyes focused on the ball so you can gauge where you need to position yourself to hit your return. Often, players will run to where the ball is going to bounce and then find themselves too close to the ball to extend their racket and make a smooth stroke. You should try to keep your head as still as possible and your shoulders level, and keep your eye on the ball all the way into your racket strings.

The Coil

To generate power, the best players use a motion that resembles a cobra before it pounces on its prey. In this case, it is the rotation of the upper and lower body and the whiplike action of the racket that produces what is often called the *coil*.

Start by turning your body so that your shoulders are perpendicular to the net. (This is assuming that you have time to do this; if your opponent's shot has more pace on it, you may have to hit from an open stance without turning your shoulders. This stance is covered later in this chapter). The rotation starts in your hips and moves upward to

Turning your body

Keep nonracket arm perpendicular to shoulder.

your chest and then your shoulders. Your racket arm and racket rotate back to complete the first part of the coil.

Your non-racket arm provides an important component of your swing as well. Many players keep this arm out in front of them as they turn, at an angle close to perpendicular from the shoulders. This helps keep the ball at a comfortable distance away from the body as you prepare to hit your forehand, and helps produce a balanced, fluid stroke. Another way to stop yourself from getting too close to the ball is to make sure your back foot is planted inside the point where you will make contact with the ball.

As the ball approaches and after you have rotated your shoulders, your wrist should be cocked back with your elbow bent and fairly close to your body. Viewed from above, the head of your racket should be on the continuation of an imaginary line extending from your lead shoulder through your back shoulder.

From this stance—called a *closed stance*—your weight should be mostly on your back foot. Your knees should be slightly bent. As you begin your swing, your front foot should move forward toward the net as you transfer your weight from your back foot to your front foot. Try not to step across your body with your front foot, or you will be too close to the ball and may not be able to get out of your own way when you make contact.

From an open stance, in which your shoulders are basically parallel to the baseline and you are facing the net, make sure to keep the ball outside your back foot (the right foot for a right-handed player) to avoid swinging across your body.

As you prepare to swing, you will want to keep your wrist cocked back at about 90 degrees, and keep it locked in this position through your swing. This will keep the racket head steady as you make contact with the ball. The racket handle should lead the way, with the butt end of the handle pointing at the ball at the beginning of your swing. Your elbow and forearm should form another angle that is about 90 degrees. As you swing through, your hips, chest, and shoulders will whip the racket head through the ball.

Note: Many professional players seem to be jumping as they hit their forehands. This actually results from the powerful leg drive they get as they push off the ground and into their swing, which then carries them off the ground. It is best to concentrate on developing a fluid stroke by keeping both of your feet on the ground and pushing up and through the ball with your legs as you swing.

Making Contact

Probably the biggest weakness of younger or novice players is an inability to make contact with the ball at the same point during each groundstroke. Most of the time this point will be slightly out in front of your body; the exact range will vary with each player. The key is to be comfortable and balanced whenever you are hitting a forehand, with your weight moving forward and driving through the ball instead of being off-balance and stabbing or poking at the ball. With practice, you will gain a sense of what works for you.

One thing to remember is to let your nonracket arm work in tandem with your racket arm. As you swing through, try to keep your nonracket arm steady as you rotate, so that it winds up moving with your stroke. Both arms should almost trace an arc in tandem. This will give you a fluid stroke.

TOPSPIN FOREHAND

An effective Topspin forehand can be the strongest weapon in your arsenal. It is a shot that can put your opponent at a disadvantage by keeping her pinned at the baseline during rallies, or it can win points outright when used as a passing shot. Whether you hit with one hand or two, all players need to develop a Topspin forehand to compete successfully.

Grip

An Eastern, Semi-Western, or Western grip will enable you to put top-spin on your forehand shots. For a complete description of these grips, plus a diagram of where to place your hand on the racket handle, consult Chapter 4.

Start your swing low, below the level of the ball. You will be swinging up and through the ball in an inside-out motion, which means starting with the racket closer to your body and finishing with it slightly further away from your body.

Your weight should be mostly on your back foot. Keep your wrist locked in a 90-degree position as described earlier. As you start your forward swing, the butt end of your racket should be pointing directly at the ball. The swing should be a continuous loop: back and up on the backswing, then down, up, and accelerating through the ball.

You should make contact with the ball in front of your front foot. Keeping your wrist locked in position, transfer your weight from your back foot to your front foot and swing up and through the ball as if you were applying a brush stroke. Follow through so that the racket head ends up above your nonhitting shoulder.

The Topspin forehand: Ready position at baseline

The Topspin forehand: turning shoulder toward net

The Topspin forehand: coil, weight on back foot

The Topspin forehand: contact, weight on stride foot

The Topspin forehand: follow-through

FOREHAND SLICE

With the emphasis on power tennis over the years, the Forehand slice is rarely used by elite players. But it can be a valuable shot to have in your repertoire, and a big headache for your opponents. All players should master backspin and topspin on both the forehand and backhand sides to add variety to their games.

The Forehand slice will bounce much lower than a Topspin forehand. It can be used to block back a fast serve, or to hit an approach shot that will force your opponent to bend down and hit up on the ball to get it over the net, creating an easy volley opportunity for you.

Grip

Probably the easiest grip to use when hitting a Forehand slice is a Continental grip, which is the same grip you use for volleying. However, you can still hit a slice shot using an Eastern Forehand grip.

In contrast to the Topspin forehand, the Forehand slice uses an outside-in motion, in which the racket begins further away from your body and finishes closer to your body. Start your racket above the level of the ball, so you are swinging slightly down on the ball. The racket face should be slightly open, which means it is tilted back a little.

From a closed position—shoulders perpendicular to the baseline—you should make contact with the ball just about even with, or a little in front of,

The Forehand slice: Ready position

The Forehand slice: high backswing

The Forehand slice: downward motion

The Forehand slice: contact

your lead shoulder. You should transfer your weight from your back foot to your front foot, just as you do when you are hitting a Topspin forehand.

With the racket still in an open position, swing through the ball with a downward motion and follow through by bringing the racket up past shoulder level.

REVERSE FOREHAND

The Forehand slice: follow-through

The Reverse forehand is a somewhat unorthodox shot that can bail you out of trouble in a rally. It can be used to hit a cross-court down-the-line winner from off the court, or topspin lob.

The reason this shot is unorthodox is because it goes against some of the rules for a regular forehand. For one, you usually hit this shot

The open-stance forehand: footwork

The open-stance forehand: contact zone

The open-stance forehand: follow-through

from an open stance, rather than a closed stance. You also make contact with the ball a little behind your back foot instead of in front of it. And your follow-through should bring your racket up and over your racket shoulder instead of your opposite shoulder.

The Reverse forehand is an advanced shot that should be practiced only after the Topspin and Slice forehands have been mastered.

8

THE BACKHAND

THE BASICS

Getting Ready

As we discussed in the section on hitting the forehand, your preparation to hit a backhand begins with a small hop, often called a ready hop, timed to the moment when your opponent hits the ball. This will prevent you from being caught flat-footed and get your leg muscles ready to react. Keep your eyes on your opponent and on the ball; she may be doing something that telegraphs where she is going to hit the ball.

Once you have identified the ball coming to your backhand side, keep your eyes focused on the ball so you can gauge where you need to position yourself to hit your return. Often, players will run to where the ball is going to bounce and then find themselves too close to the ball to extend their racket and make a smooth stroke. This is especially important if you hit a two-handed backhand, which requires more upper-body coordination since you are using both arms to hit the ball. You should try to keep your head as still as possible and your shoulders level, and keep your eye on the ball all the way into your racket strings.

The backhand: preparation

The backhand: the tap tip, chin to shoulder

The Coil

Because you are hitting across your body when you hit a backhand, it can almost be easier to produce the coil that generates power on your stroke.

Start by turning your body so that your shoulders are perpendicular to the net. Your weight should be mostly on your back foot, and your elbows and knees should be slightly bent. If you are hitting a one-handed backhand, keep your nonracket hand on the throat of the racket to provide stability and balance during your backswing.

With your weight still mostly on your back foot, bring the racket back so that the head is above the level of your shoulders. This high backswing gives you several options: you can swing through and hit a flat shot, swing down and up through the loop and hit a topspin shot, or swing in a more downward motion and hit a Backhand slice or drop shot. Your lead shoulder should be in a closed position, which means that if you are standing on the baseline, it should be pointing almost parallel to the baseline.

Tip: To reinforce the turning of your body from the backswing through the follow-through, use the *tap* tip: Tap your chin to your front shoulder as you bring your racket back—this ensures you are fully coiled and ready to swing through. After you make contact, let your chin tap the inside of your back shoulder as you swing through—this ensures a full follow-through.

Making Contact

As you begin your swing and transfer your weight from your back foot to your front foot, the butt end of your racket should be pointed directly at the ball. At this point, you can release your nonracket hand from the throat of the racket, splitting your hands before you make contact with the ball.

Where contact is made with the ball may depend on which type of backhand you are hitting. For a Backhand slice, you usually want to make contact with the ball about even with your front foot. For a Topspin backhand, you may want to meet the ball a little bit in front of your front foot.

Hitting From an Open Stance

There will be many occasions, for example, on a return of a first serve hit with pace, when you will not have time to turn your body to prepare for a backhand. In these situations, you will need to hit from an open stance, in which your body is essentially facing the net and your back leg is close to parallel with your front leg.

The open-stance backhand: Ready position

The open-stance backhand: turning upper body

The open-stance backhand: backswing

The open-stance backhand: forward swing

The key to remember when hitting an open-stance backhand is that you still need to rotate your hips, torso, and shoulders to get power into the shot. The difference is that you are stepping out wide with your back leg (your left leg if you are right-handed) instead of keeping it behind you. Use the back leg as a stabilizer and swing through the ball as you would normally. The advantage is that on your follow-through, you are back in the Ready position for your opponent's next shot without having to turn your body.

The Backhand slice: contact point   **The Backhand slice: follow-through**

BACKHAND SLICE

The Backhand slice is an all-purpose shot that can be used whether you are in control of the point or on the defensive. It is an effective approach shot when you want to close out a rally at the net, or when you are on the run and you want to buy yourself a little extra time to get back into position. It can be hit comfortably and without too much adjustment whether the ball is coming in high or low. In other words, it is a shot all players should know how to hit.

What you are aiming to do when you hit a Backhand slice is to take pace off the ball and, by hitting it with exaggerated backspin, cause the ball to bounce low or skid, forcing your opponent to reach down and hit up on the ball, giving you a chance to play a weak return.

The best grip to use to hit a Backhand slice is the Continental grip. (See Chapter 4 for illustrations and descriptions of different kinds of racket grips).

Starting in a closed position—shoulders and feet in line, perpendicular to the baseline—turn your body even more so that you feel as though your back is almost facing the net. This additional motion will stop you from opening up your shoulders too soon and will allow you to hit through the ball and produce some power. Try to have your elbow pointing directly at the ball.

The swing for a Backhand slice is down and through the ball, with the racket face slightly open, which means it is tilted back a little. For a slice that is flat and skids when it hits the court, take your racket back just a little above the level of the ball. For a slice with more exaggerated spin that will die when it hits the court surface, bring your racket back a little higher before swinging down and through the ball.

The point of contact can vary, depending on your opponent's shot. You can play the ball low and on the rise, as it comes up off the court, or higher if the shot has topspin and bounces higher. In either situation, your stroke should be similar, and the racket should meet the ball just in front of your lead shoulder.

The follow-through is crucial to the success of the Backhand slice. Many players punch the shot and cut short their follow-throughs, which usually results in a shot that lands short and without much pace and can give an opponent an immediate advantage. Follow through all the way so that your racket arm is fully extended and the racket head is at least at shoulder level.

TOPSPIN BACKHAND–TWO-HANDER

Like the Topspin forehand, the Topspin backhand is a required shot for players who want to compete successfully. If your backhand is not as strong as your forehand, an opponent will spot this weakness right away and exploit it. If you are like many players who find it easier to master the forehand shots, you may want to spend more time working on your backhand to make sure it is up to par.

Probably the most common grip for a two-handed backhand is to hold the top hand (left hand if are right-handed) with an Eastern

The Topspin backhand: coil

The Topspin backhand: contact zone

The Topspin backhand: follow-through

grip, and the bottom hand with a Continental grip. (See Chapter 4 for illustrations and descriptions of different kinds of racket grips). The Eastern grip helps provide power with the palm of your hand whipping the racket through the stroke, while the Continental grip adds control as well as the ability to hit a slice or volley when using just the bottom hand.

Start your shoulder turn early, before the ball bounces. Your shoulders should be perpendicular to the baseline, with your weight on your back foot. Bring the racket back and through in a continuous loop: back and up on the backswing, then down, up, and accelerating through the ball. This motion will produce topspin on the ball. As with the forehand, swinging through the ball with a more downward motion at impact will pro-

The two-handed backhand: start swing low

The two-handed backhand: swing low to high

The two-handed backhand: contact zone   **The two-handed backhand: follow-through**

duce slice, or backspin, while swinging through on a level plane will produce a flat shot.

As the ball bounces up off the court, turn your shoulders and hips toward the ball and pull the racket through as you shift your weight forward to your front foot. You should make contact with the ball a little bit in front of your front foot.

Make sure to follow through completely, with the racket head winding up above the level of your head and shoulders. Let your back foot follow through and end up even with your front foot, so you are squarely facing the net and ready to hit your next return.

ONE-HANDED BACKHAND

While many younger players prefer to hit a two-handed backhand to generate more power, the one-handed backhand is a useful shot to learn. With the one-hander, you can hit a variety of shots—topspin, backspin, flat, drop shot—more easily than with the two-hander. This can add versatility to your game and keep your opponent guessing during a match.

The most common grip used for a one-handed backhand is the Eastern grip, which gives you the flexibility to hit the ball flat, or with backspin or topspin, with small adjustments. More advanced players

The one-handed backhand: nonracket arm trailing the racket arm

The one-handed backhand: follow-through

The one-handed backhand: finish

may want to experiment with a Western grip, which can produce heavy topspin on your shots. (See Chapter 4 for illustrations and descriptions of different kinds of racket grips).

From your Ready position, hold the racket with both hands. Your nonhitting hand should hold the racket shaft lightly just below the racket head. This will aid in keeping your racket in a steady position as you begin your backswing. Start your shoulder turn early, before the ball bounces. Your shoulders should be perpendicular to the baseline, with your weight on your back foot.

Bring the racket back and through in a continuous loop: back and up on the backswing, then down, up, and accelerating through the ball. This motion will produce topspin on the ball. As with the forehand, swinging through the ball with a more downward motion at impact will produce slice, or backspin, while swinging through on a level plane will produce a flat shot.

As the ball bounces up off the court, turn your shoulders and hips toward the ball and pull the racket through as you shift your weight forward to your front foot. Release your nonhitting hand from the racket before you make contact, preferably as you start your forward swing, or wherever you feel comfortable. You should make contact with the ball a little bit in front of your front foot.

Make sure to follow through completely, with the racket head winding up above the level of your head and shoulders. Let your back foot follow through and end up even with your front foot, so you are squarely facing the net and ready to hit your next return.

THE SERVE

9

It is no exaggeration to say that the serve is the most important shot in tennis. Why? Because it is the one shot on which you can completely control where the ball is going, how fast, and with what type of spin. You start the point with the serve and are able to dictate play immediately; it is your chance to force your opponent into a defensive position right away.

THE BASICS

There are several parts to the serve, but the main thing to remember is that all the parts have to blend together to form one smooth, continuous motion. Your goal should always be to hit the serve—or any of your strokes—with as consistent a motion as possible each time.

Types of Serves

There are three basic types of serves: *flat, slice,* and *kick.* The motion and grip necessary to produce each one is described below. You should try to master all three, or at least familiarize yourself with all three with the goal of eventually being able to use them in a match. Each can add variety to your service game and give your opponent one more thing to think about when you are serving.

Grip

Probably the best grip to use when hitting your serve is the Eastern forehand grip (see Chapter 4 for a complete description and illustration of the Eastern forehand grip). The Eastern grip will allow you to hit a flat serve, slice serve, and spin or kick serve without changing your grip.

Some players prefer to use a Continental grip on their serve, which makes it easier to serve and volley since the Continental grip is the same grip you use when you are hitting volleys.

The serve motion: preparation

The serve motion: rest the racket against the nonracket hand, ball in hand

Stance/Preparation

Serving motions can vary from player to player; no two will be exactly the same. Still, learning the fundamentals will help you to develop your own style. To begin, stand slightly to the right of the center mark on the baseline with your front foot at about a 45-degree angle to the baseline. Your back foot should be almost parallel to your front foot, or even close to perpendicular to the baseline. Your feet should be about shoulder-width apart.

Hold the ball in your nonracket hand and lightly rest the racket against the nonracket hand, at a height that feels comfortable between waist and chest level. Keep your racket hand relaxed.

There are two basic foot motions used during a serve. In the first, you bring your back foot up to a spot just behind or next to your front foot while your toss is in the air, and push off with both feet as you thrust upward to meet the ball. In the second, you keep your feet in basically the same position throughout the toss and push off to meet the ball from the same position.

Some players like to shift their weight from their back foot to their front while they are preparing to toss the ball, which produces a kind of rocking motion. Experiment until you find what is most comfortable for you.

Ball Toss

Holding the ball with your fingertips with your palm facing upward, extend your arm so that when you release the ball your arm is fully straightened. As a general rule, let go of the ball at about eye level, and follow the ball's flight upward with your eyes while tracking the ball with your tossing hand—your hand should complete the tossing motion above your head.

Finding the right height to make your ball toss is a trial-and-error process. Take the time to work on your toss so that you feel comfortable hitting your serve and can toss the ball to the same spot each time.

Swing Motion

Instructors often say that hitting a serve should feel like you are throwing the racket as you would throw a baseball or softball, and this is an accurate

The serve motion: ball toss

analogy. Not unlike a pitcher in baseball, the success of your serve depends on your arms, shoulders, hips, legs, and feet all moving in one smooth, continuous motion to generate power and maintain consistency.

Your backswing should begin before you release the ball on your toss, so that by the time the ball is in the air, your racket arm is fully extended behind you. Your knees should be bent at this point, as you prepare to launch yourself into the shot. Swing your racket through as if you are throwing the racket head at the ball in an upward motion. Your racket arm should be fully extended when you make contact, with your hand and wrist leading the way and accelerating the racket head through the point of contact with the ball. At this point, your legs should be straight as you extend your body toward the ball.

Making Contact

Where and how you make contact with the ball will determine what kind of serve you hit of the three we mentioned above:

- To hit a flat serve, the racket should hit the ball squarely in the center, with little or no upward or sideward motion. If you picture your service motion using the hands of a clock, you should make contact with the ball at about 12:00. You will usually be able to hit a flat serve with more power than a spin serve, but you also may have more difficulty controlling it.

- To hit a slice serve, toss the ball a little in front and to the right of your front foot. Your goal is to make contact with the upper-right portion of the ball, which will put sidespin on the serve. Try to hit the ball between 2:00 and 3:00.
- To hit a spin, or kick serve, you want to brush up the back side of the ball, much as you would on a topspin forehand or backhand. Your toss should be directly overhead, or even a little to the left of that point. Contact should be made with the ball at between 12:00 and 1:00. A kick serve will produce a high bounce, making for a difficult return for your opponent.

Follow-Through/Recovery

After you have made contact with the ball, your follow-through will carry you over the baseline and into the court. Your front foot will usually land first, followed by your back foot (your right foot if you are right-handed) which will come forward alongside your front foot. Your racket arm should continue downward and across your body, past your opposite leg.

You should immediately get into your Ready position (see Chapter 5) to prepare for your opponent's return. You should never be off-balance during your follow-through; if you are, you need to work on your service motion to correct any flaws.

TIPS

Second, then First

Spend at least as much time practicing your second serve as you do your first serve. Experiment with different spins, and when you have mastered one or more, try to swing as hard on your second serve as you did on your first. This will create more spin, and, once you have increased your confidence in your second serve, it will give you more confidence in your first serve.

The Wider, the Better

You should always try to serve away from your opponent, so that she will have to extend herself to reach the ball and (you hope) make a weak return. A good way to do this while increasing your chances at hitting a winner off her return is to serve wide and force her off the court to make her return. It sounds simple, but it is sound advice that works most of the time. Even if her return is strong, you will be able to make your next shot into the open court and force her to run it down.

The flat serve

The slice: immediately after contact, moving forward

Fall Forward

To add more pace to your serves, toss the ball up and out a little farther over the court. You will still be extending upward to make contact, but you will be moving forward and generating more momentum. Your body should almost feel as if it is falling toward the court.

DRILLS

- To familiarize yourself with the service motion, take a tennis ball and, standing on the service line, play catch with someone standing on the other service line. Concentrate on throwing overhand (as opposed to sidearm or three-quarters) and using a smooth, continuous motion without using too much wrist motion.
- Once you have developed a smooth serving motion, work on your accuracy by setting up a serve target. This can be done by simply drawing a chalk box about two feet by two feet above the height of the net on a practice wall or backboard. Or, you can lean a broom handle or other long object against the net so that it sticks up about a foot or two above the net. Aim to either side of the object, and your serves will begin to find the service court with frequency (you may knock the object over every once in a while, but that's a good sign too).

- With an ample supply of tennis balls, keep score by how many serves you put in the court. There are infinite variations to this game. For instance, you can use just first serves, giving yourself a point for each one you put in and giving your imaginary opponent a point for each one you miss. Score it as you would a normal game (15-0, 15-15, 15-30, etc.). Or, you can mark off an area of the service court for your second serve and give yourself a point each time you hit that spot. Or, you can give yourself a point each time you serve successfully down the middle on the deuce side and wide to the ad side. The multiple variations, plus the fact that you can do it on your own, make this a great drill.
- To get more work on your serve with a live opponent, play games to 10 or 11 points with one player serving the whole time. Vary the rules so that in some games you are only using second serves, or are only serving down the middle, or are required to serve and volley on every point. This will give you more practice on the different aspects of your serve than if you were playing regular-length games.

MARTINA HINGIS

One could say that Martina Hingis was destined to be a tennis star almost from birth, or from the moment her mother decided to name her after Martina Navratilova, a fellow Czechoslovakian who stood atop the tennis world in the 1980s and 1990s. It took years of hard work and determination, but eventually young Martina began to follow in the footsteps of her famous namesake. By the time she was 12, she was already one of the best junior (under-18) players in the world, and at 13 won the Wimbledon and French Open junior singles titles against players several years older.

With no mountains left to climb in the junior ranks, Hingis decided to turn professional in the fall of 1994, when she turned 14. Her timing was unfortunate, though, as the women's tennis tour had just instituted rules to restrict the number of tournaments players could enter until they turned 16. This ruling came in the wake of heightened concern over young players "burning out" or being unable to cope with the pressures of playing on the pro tour, with the plight of Jennifer Capriati being the most celebrated example. In the case of Hingis, however, the concern was largely unnecessary, as her background and upbringing were a model of how to succeed while keeping one's feet firmly planted on the ground.

Though Hingis's mother, Melanie, a former player herself, introduced Martina to tennis at a very young age (2, according to some accounts), she encouraged her to try other sports as well. As a result, Martina became an avid skier, swimmer, and horseback rider as well as developing into a world-class tennis player. In addition to adding variety to her athletic pursuits, these activities directly improved her tennis game by helping her to develop coordination and balance. By the time she turned pro, she was already known as one of the most agile and graceful players on the tour.

What was significant about Hingis's upbringing was that it reinforced the notion that there was a whole world that existed outside the tennis court, even though tennis was where she would ultimately make her career. To this day, at many of the tour stops around the world, she still finds time to go horseback riding or in-line skating on her days off.

Recognizing that there is more to life than tennis has certainly not hurt Martina Hingis's results. By the end of 2001 she owned 13 Grand Slam tournament titles (5 singles, 8 doubles) and had earned more than $16 million in prize money. Far from being a victim of her own success, she has continued to adapt and adjust as the level of competition on the women's tour has risen in leaps and bounds.

10
VOLLEYING

Tennis players are usually described as serve-and-volleyers or baseliners, but the truth is that everyone needs to be able to play from the baseline and everyone needs to be able to volley. Whatever your style of play and ability level, you need to master all facets of the game so that you can adapt to any situation that occurs during a match. Unfortunately, volleying is an integral part of the game of tennis that is too often ignored by young players who feel uncomfortable coming to the net.

A strong net game can set you apart from other players who may otherwise be comparable to you in ability. By attacking the net, you can force your opponent out of her game and cause errors that will give you free points. No matter how strong your groundstrokes are, it is much harder to hit a clean winner from the baseline than it is when you are at the net.

MENTAL APPROACH

Attacking the net can be a feast-or-famine proposition. You can look great when you are volleying an angled winner into the corner, or you can look helpless when you give your opponent an easy opening and she whips a passing shot right by you. The point is to not get discouraged; if your strategy is to go to the net frequently, understand that you will not win every point, but you will win a good enough percentage to put yourself in position to win the match.

Always pay attention to what your opponent does when you are at the net. Does she hit a lob instead of trying a passing shot? Does she hold back on her groundstrokes, or does she hit them harder? Does she tend to go crosscourt or down the line? Which is her weaker side? Make a mental note of these and adjust your play to take advantage of any weaknesses.

THE BASICS

Grip

Since you often do not have time to change your grip while you are at the net reacting to your opponent's shot, the best grip to use for volleying is usually a Continental grip (see Chapter 4 for a complete description and illustration of the Continental grip).

The Continental grip lets you hit a forehand volley, backhand volley, or overhead without changing your hand position on the racket. It also makes it easy to put backspin on the ball when you want to hit a drop volley.

Net Approach and Positioning

Your approach shot is the first component of your net approach, and possibly the most important. If your approach shot is too short, not placed well, or otherwise gives your opponent time to find an opening and pass you, you can be the best volleyer in the world and it won't make any difference.

We will focus on the three options you have on your approach shot: crosscourt, down the line, and down the middle. In some situations, you can come to the net after hitting a lob or drop shot, but those will be covered later in this book.

Your goal with any approach shot is to put yourself in position to close out the point by cutting down the angles for your opponent's passing shot and limiting her options. It is important to remember that your first volley does not necessarily have to be a winner, but that it should at the very least put you in position to end the point with the second (or third) volley.

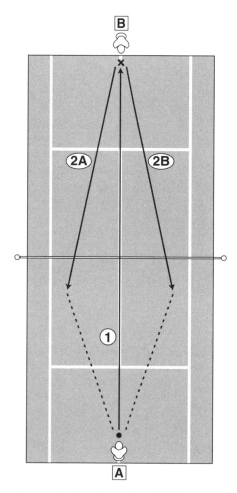

Approach shot down the middle

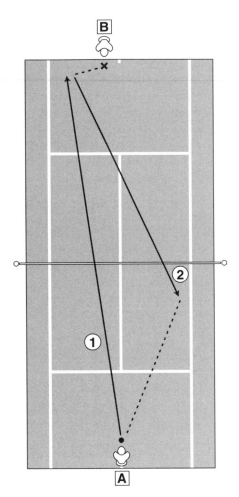

Approach shot, deep baseline left

Some basic rules to remember about approach shots:

1. Where you are on the court when you hit your approach shot usually determines the direction where you should hit it. An approach shot down the middle will give your opponent fewer angles to work with, but should be used when you are hitting a ball from the middle of the court. If you hit down the middle from either corner, you will have too much ground to cover to get in position at the middle of the net.

2. Similar to Rule 1, if you hit a crosscourt or down-the-line approach shot from one corner of the court, you will have more distance to cover to get in position at the net. If you are late getting there, your opponent will have an opening to exploit.

3. A crosscourt or down-the-line approach shot is often best used when you have your opponent at a disadvantage in a rally and you can force a weak return with a well-angled shot, or perhaps hit an outright winner.

4. A slice shot, hit with underspin, is the classic approach shot, as it will bounce low and force your opponent to hit up on the ball and increase your chances of getting an easy volley that you can put away.

5. Remember that the faster you hit your approach shot, the quicker the ball will reach your opponent—and the quicker her shot will come back at you. Unless you are going for a winner, it is almost better to take some pace off your approach shot to give yourself time to get to the net and in position.

A general rule of thumb on net positioning is that you should be able to reach a crosscourt or down-the-line passing shot by taking one step either way and reaching out with your racket. You should be positioned about six feet from the net so that you can get back quickly to cover a possible lob by your opponent.

Ready Position for Volleying

Balance and footwork on volleys is probably more important than it is when you are hitting groundstrokes (though it certainly is important then, too), simply because you have to react much quicker when you are volleying, and an error in positioning will be more difficult, if not impossible, to correct in time.

Volleying: the Ready position

Your goal is to be in the Ready position when you are preparing to hit your volley. (See Chapter 5 for a description and illustrations). The fundamentals of the Ready position are as follows:

- Feet a little more than shoulder width apart
- Leaning slightly forward with your back straight
- Knees bent slightly
- Feet firmly on the ground, with most of your weight on the balls of your feet.

Split Step

To assume the Ready position when you are approaching the net, you will need to do a Split step, which will widen your stance and get you ready to react and move quickly to either side without losing your balance.

The Split step is actually more a small hop than a step. What you are doing is splitting your feet apart about three or

Volleying: the Split step

four inches farther than they are when you start. The key to the Split step is to time it so that your feet touch down at the moment your opponent's racket makes contact with the ball. You should land with your knees bent and your body leaning slightly forward, with most of your weight on your toes. This will get you ready to move to the left or right, depending on where the ball is hit.

Since you are moving forward into your Split step, instead of being in a more stationary position as you would for a groundstroke, it may take some practice to get comfortable with this movement. Do not try to completely stop your forward momentum when you do your Split step; you can lose your balance this way and fall forward. On the other hand, you want to try not to hit a volley while you are running forward, as you will sacrifice control. You want to maintain your forward momentum while slowing enough so that you are in control and not in danger of running into the net.

As you make your Split step and prepare to hit your volley, remember to keep your racket head up at eye level with your nonhitting hand on the throat of the racket to provide support.

Drill

Have your partner hit you a mid-range ball and hit your approach shot. Do your Split step at the service line and volley the return, then have your partner feed you a second volley. Repeat this pattern several times, first with only forehand volleys, then with backhand volleys, then alternating. Practice first with approaches and first volleys down the line, followed by a crosscourt volley, then change the pattern.

FOOTWORK

Getting Down and Dirty

You hear tennis coaches say it all the time: "Bend your knees!" This is good advice for when you are volleying a low ball. It may seem logical to just bend a little at the waist and reach down with your racket to hit a low volley. Particularly if you are fatigued, this can be an easy way out. But the only way to guarantee power and accuracy—and to ensure that you will even get the shot over the net—is to bend at the knee and really go down and dig the ball out.

Watch a top player like Venus Williams hit low volleys, and sometimes it seems she will get so low that she will touch the ground with her back knee. This is a way of getting in position to meet the ball on her terms, so that she can control it and put the volley where she wants.

When moving forward toward the ball to hit a low volley, both knees should be bent with the back knee (left knee if you are right-handed and hitting a backhand volley) bent slightly lower to the ground. Your upper body should be as straight as possible. Try to keep the racket face above the level of your wrist and slightly open (tilted back) to put backspin on your volley.

Reach for It

Another popular saying among tennis instructors is that "you go to the ball with your feet, not with your racket." This means that you need to use your feet and legs to get in position so that you can put your racket to its best use.

How does this apply to volleying? Well, unless your opponent is very obliging, she will not hit every shot directly at you while you are at the net. So, when you have to reach to either side to get to the ball, you will need to move your feet to put yourself in position to hit a strong volley return. There are two ways to do this:

- Cross over with the foot that is away from the side the ball is on—your left foot if you are right-handed and hitting a forehand volley, or your right foot if you are hitting a backhand volley. This is an instinctive move that feels comfortable; however, it leaves you in a closed position and makes for a slightly longer recovery back to the ready position.
- Step toward the ball with the foot that is closest to the ball—your right foot if you are right-handed and hitting a forehand volley, or your left foot if you are hitting a backhand volley. This may seem a little awkward at first, but once you master it, you will find yourself able to recover quickly for the next volley.

Drill

Stand at the service line while your partner stands at the other service line. Put the ball in play and keep it in play using only volleys. This will help you to work on your footwork and balance as well as your anticipation. Make sure to perform your split step as your opponent makes contact.

TYPES OF VOLLEYS

Forehand

For the forehand volley, as for all volleys, you want to forget about taking a big backswing and instead concentrate on hitting the ball with a short, compact motion. In most cases you will not have time to fully rotate your hips and shoulders, as you would when hitting a forehand groundstroke.

From your Ready position using a Continental grip and with your nonhitting hand lightly grasping the throat of the racket, cock your wrist back slightly and bring your racket to the forehand side as you turn your shoulders in that direction. Your racket should not go back behind the plane of your shoulders, but should instead be in front of you at an angle. Your arm should be

The forehand volley

slightly bent as you prepare to make contact with the ball. Your swing motion will depend on the height of the ball, but in general it is a good idea to hold the racket in a slightly open (tilted-back) position and swing in a downward motion, which will help you control the volley by creating backspin on the ball.

You should make contact with the ball in front of you, and use a shorter follow-through than you do on your forehand groundstroke. The reason for this is that since you are using your opponent's shot to create pace, you do not have to generate as much power yourself. On a softly hit ball, you may want to use a longer follow-through to generate more pace on the ball.

As soon as you have hit your volley, immediately return to the Ready position to prepare for your opponent's next shot.

One-Handed Backhand

The technique for hitting a one-handed backhand volley is very similar to that used to hit a forehand volley: little or no backswing, compact swing motion, shoulders turned toward the side, back straight, and the arm slightly bent as you prepare to make contact with the ball. Let your nonhitting hand leave the racket as you move to hit the ball and extend behind you to provide balance during the shot.

Contact should be made in front of your body, with your arm still bent and the racket in a slightly open position to enable you to put backspin on your shot. Your follow-through should be short.

Two-Handed Backhand

For a two-handed backhand volley, use the same steps as the one-handed backhand with one difference: you will keep both hands on the racket instead of releasing your upper hand. The Continental grip is the best grip to use on the lower hand for volleys, particularly if you have to reach wide for a backhand volley and need to release the top hand from the racket.

The two-handed backhand volley is a common shot used by younger players who have not yet developed the strength to hit a one-handed volley. It can be a difficult shot to use against players who hit the ball harder, so you may want to work on developing a one-handed backhand volley as your game improves and the level of competition rises.

The two-handed backhand volley: short backswing

The two-handed backhand volley: contact

The low backhand volley

Half Volley

Usually a defensive shot, the half volley is your answer when your opponent hits a ball that is down near your feet and is too low for you to volley in the air, but too close to you to take a full swing and hit a groundstroke. So, you end up hitting the ball on a short hop, which makes it difficult to generate much power or placement.

Nevertheless, you should look at the half volley as an opportunity to keep yourself in the point.

The key is to keep the ball as low to the ground and as deep as possible into your opponent's court. To do this, you need to stay low yourself. Bend your knees while keeping your upper body close to vertical—in other words, do not bend over from the waist to reach the ball—and move forward into the ball as you would for a regular volley. Experienced players will bend their knees so that their back knee—the right leg for a right-hander hitting a forehand half volley—almost touches the ground.

Keep the face of your racket vertical or slightly closed. This will prevent you from popping the ball up in the air and giving your opponent an easy put-away opportunity. Your backswing should be minimal, since you usually only have time to get your racket to the correct side. Keep your wrist firm as you meet the ball, and make contact with the ball slightly in front of your body. Follow through after you make contact to ensure you get enough depth on the shot.

Drop Volley

This is a very useful shot that can take an opponent by surprise and lead to a clean winner or, often, set up a clean winner on your next shot. It can also frustrate an opponent by making her expend more energy than she may want to, particularly in the late stages of a match.

The key thing to remember about the drop volley is that you are trying to take pace off the ball instead of trying to create pace. So, while you are basically using the same motion that you would for a regular volley—no backswing, short follow-through, open-faced racket to produce backspin—you will have to practice, in essence, deadening the ball as it hits your racket strings. You can do this by relaxing your grip slightly as you make contact, and by cutting down on the ball even more than usual to create more backspin and less forward motion.

The drop volley will probably take more practice to perfect than many other shots, but the reward will be worth it, as you will have yet another weapon in your arsenal. At the very least, it will keep your opponent guessing.

Swinging Volley

The swinging volley is a difficult shot to master, but also a shot that can demoralize an opponent when hit correctly.

The swinging volley works best with an Eastern or Semi-Western grip, as if you are hitting a high forehand. It is usually hit from the middle of the court as you move forward from the baseline. You have to approach the swinging volley as you would a big forehand: big backswing, accelerating the racket into the point of contact, and a big follow-through. Be patient when you practice it, and concentrate first on getting it over the net with pace before you try to place it in the corners.

VOLLEYING TIPS

Take a Picture

Pretend that someone is taking your picture while you are hitting the volley. This will make you concentrate harder on your form, and will result in better, more controlled volleys.

Grip It and Rip It

To add more depth and punch to your volleys, squeeze the racket handle firmly just before you make contact with the ball. You will find that you will hit the ball more cleanly and firmly.

Bottom First

On your follow-through, try to lead with the bottom edge of the racket head so that it ends up pointing at where you want the ball to go. This will help you with placement, and will also ensure that you have put some backspin on the ball so that it skids or bounces low when it hits the court surface.

"Catch" the Ball

To simulate the volley stroke, put down your racket and have your partner hit the ball to you. Catch it with your racket hand. This motion uses about the same backswing—in other words, hardly any— as that used in a typical forehand volley.

11
SPECIALTY SHOTS

DROP SHOT

Basically, the drop shot is a shot that you want to drop just over the other side of the net, so that your opponent has to race toward the net to retrieve it. This frequently puts her out of position and leaves the court open for you to hit a winner off her return.

The drop shot is an effective ploy that is too often ignored by players who feel it necessary to hit every shot as if they are trying to knock down a brick wall. Sometimes, all it takes is losing to an opponent who hits a lot of drop shots to drive home the point.

When to Hit It

This will depend on the situation, but you generally have a better opening if a) your opponent is in the backcourt, preferably on or behind the baseline; b) has hit a playable shot, i.e., one that is not deep or hit with a lot of pace; and c) you are inside the baseline.

How to Hit It

The key is to catch the ball on the rise, as it is traveling upward after hitting the ground. Your swing should be high to low, with your racket face open. The combination of the rising ball and the open-faced racket swung in a downward motion will create more backspin and make the ball die when it lands on the other side of the net.

Where to Hit It

The best drop shots are angled toward either sideline rather than over the center of the net. An angled drop shot will force your opponent out of position and leave the court open for you to hit a winner on your next shot.

OVERHEAD

The overhead is one of tennis's purely offensive shots, and is almost always hit from the forecourt. This means you are on the offensive and are in a position to win the point. Therefore, it is important to hit your overheads with pace and, above all, accuracy, to produce either a clean winner or a shot that keeps your opponent on the defensive.

Surprisingly enough, the overhead appears to be one of the easier shots in tennis, but actually is the one that many amateur and club players fail to master. Having a strong overhead can be worth several points per match, which can be the difference between winning and losing.

When to Hit It

Any looping of high ball that is going to land in the forecourt (the area between the service line and the net) should be hit before it bounces. This will give your opponent less time to get back into position, and will give you more angle to choose from. Balls that are going to land in the backcourt near the baseline should usually be played on the bounce.

How to Hit It

Start in the Ready position (see Chapter 5): hands in front, racket pointing forward, feet slightly wider than shoulder width apart, knees slightly flexed, leaning forward but with a straight back.

As the ball goes up and you determine its pace and depth, turn sideways and begin to track the ball, with your racket back and your nonracket arm extended upward. A mistake many players make is to face the net while preparing to hit an overhead, a stance that can rob them of power and accuracy since it uses too much arm and not enough body rotation.

As the ball drops, begin your swing as if you were hitting a serve. You should make contact with the ball slightly in front of you, with your arm at full extension and your eyes and head up. Your weight should be moving forward on the follow-through so that you end up facing the net, ready to resume the Ready position in case your opponent returns the ball.

The overhead: turning sideways

The overhead: following the ball with non-racket hand

The overhead: contact

The overhead: follow-through

Where to Hit It

If you are close to the net and your opponent is at the baseline, hit down on the ball so that it bounces inside the service line and carries over your opponent's head. If she is out of position to either side, hit to the open court or catch her off-guard by hitting behind her as she moves back into position. This is a very effective play. Hit the ball hard, but do not sacrifice accuracy. An overhead down the middle directly at your opponent can be as successful as a shot into the corner, and is much less risky.

You will obviously hit many more forehands, backhands, and serves in a normal match than you will hit overheads. But you will want to take advantage of the opportunities you get, so treat your overhead as if it were just as important as the other strokes, and give it the practice it demands. Many players shortchange working on their overheads, and pay the price during matches.

Drill

Have a coach or hitting partner feed you overheads from the opposite service line. Start at the service line and after you hit each overhead, run forward, and touch the top of the net lightly with your racket before the next ball is fed. This will force you to work on your footwork as you retreat to hit overheads, as well as build up endurance.

LOB

Whether you are playing singles or doubles, the lob is an effective defensive and offensive shot that should be a part of every player's arsenal of shots. Particularly when you are in a defensive position, a well-placed lob is easier to hit than a screaming passing shot, and often can turn the momentum of a point in your favor. At the very least, it will buy you some time to regroup and get back into a point.

When to Hit It

The obvious situation is when your opponent is at the net and you are in the backcourt. If your opponent's shot has pulled you wide of the court, the lob may be your only option. If you are stationary or the ball is within reach, it still may be the best option because your opponent may have cut off your angles for a passing shot.

How to Hit It

You should prepare to hit a lob as you would prepare to hit a normal groundstroke, except that you should bend your knees a little more and keep your body lower so that you are coming up through the ball on your swing. Remember to keep your back straight and not bend over at the waist.

When you start your swing, your racket should be well under the ball, perhaps less than a foot off the ground. The swing should be smooth—do not jab at the ball, but instead swing up and through in a fluid motion.

You should make contact with the ball in front of you with your racket in an open-faced position. Your weight should be moving forward, and your knees should be straightening as you move upward through the slot. The follow-through should end up with your racket well above your head and your chin almost touching your racket shoulder.

The lob: preparation

The lob: swing

The lob: contact

The lob: follow-through

Where to Hit It

The ideal lob will land in the backcourt, forcing your opponent to retreat from the net and hit her overhead from deeper in the court. As a rule, it is always preferable to lob to a player's backhand side, since very few players can hit a backhand overhead for winners consistently. At the very least, you will force your opponent to run around her backhand and open up more of her side of the court in case you are able to make a return.

Drill

One player starts at the baseline and the other at the net. The baseline player feeds a ball to the net player, who volleys it back or into the corner. From there, the point begins, with the baseliner hitting only lobs and the net player hitting only overheads. Keep score by giving one point to the net player for every error by the baseliner, and two points to the baseliner for every error by the net player. Play to seven (or some other agreed-on number), and then switch sides. Both players get to practice these two critical shots, but more pressure is put on the net player to be consistent with her overheads.

VENUS AND SERENA WILLIAMS

Venus and Serena Williams symbolize the new face of women's tennis—probably because they have played a large part in creating that image. Since they burst onto the pro tennis scene from their modest beginnings in gang-infested Compton, California, the sisters have redefined the way tennis is played, adding a new degree of power to the women's game that has forced the other players to follow suit or get left behind.

The road to the top has been an eventful one for the Williams family, and has not been without some bumps and potholes along the way. Their success is a testament to their talent, certainly, but equally to their work ethic and unshakable belief in themselves. Much of this was instilled by their father, Richard Williams, who has gained notoriety for some controversial comments over the years but who kept both girls focused on education as well as tennis. The result is that both young women are poised, articulate, and confident off the court, and fierce competitors on it.

Both Serena and Venus showed promise as youngsters, and their initial successes only made them hungry to improve.

"Every time someone would beat Serena, when Serena left the court, she made notes," Richard Williams told *Tennis Week* in 1998. "She wrote down: 'This is the shot I want to learn.' And she would go learn those shots, and she would come back and say, 'Get me a match with that same person.' . . . Serena learned at an early age that it's better to be smart than to be only powerful."

When it came time for his daughters to compete in junior tournaments, the standard path for aspiring players, Richard Williams took a radically different approach: he held Venus and Serena out of the junior circuit, and instead had them focus on improving their games under coach Rick Macci while schooling them at home. They practiced six hours a day, six days a week, for four years. As a result, Venus, who is two years older than Serena, was largely an unknown quantity when she made her professional debut in 1994. Playing sparingly in selected tournaments over the next two years, Venus showed potential but an obvious lack of experience. That gradually changed as she played more matches and progressed from being a player with immense talent to a player with immense talent who knew how to play the game.

Venus's breakthrough came at the 1997 U.S. Open when she reached the final before losing to Martina Hingis. Since then, the Williams sisters have won a total of eight Grand Slam trophies, a number that is sure to grow in the coming years.

12
STRATEGIES FOR PLAYING WINNING SINGLES

THE BASICS

Playing winning singles takes much more than good strokes and physical agility. You need to have a strategy, a plan that will employ your strengths, and exploit your opponent's weaknesses.

Naturally, each player you play will be different, and will pose different challenges. Some players will come at you with power, some with patience, some with slices and spins; consequently, it is difficult to use the same strategies against all players. But you will find that if you learn the following principles and put them into practice, you will be the one dictating the play to your opponent most of the time instead of the other way around. And that is the first step toward winning.

First, some general points to remember:

- If it ain't broke, don't fix it. If what you are doing is successful, don't change your tactics.
- If things are not going your way, reevaluate what you are doing— but do not overanalyze. Stay composed, but mix in some different tactics.
- Remember that all players go through peaks and valleys during a match. Your opponent may be playing like Venus Williams in the first set, but few players can maintain that level for an entire match (including Venus herself, frequently).

- Heighten your concentration on the big points (break points, set points) but do not put too much pressure on yourself. Do not try anything outlandish, but do not play tentatively. Remember that your opponent is facing the same pressure you are.
- Watch for lapses in concentration or drops in play by your opponent, and take advantage of them. These can arise from a bad call or a missed shot, and can undermine a player's confidence. Often in these cases, you can keep the ball in play and let her make the errors.
- If your strokes are betraying you and you are beginning to lose confidence, do not pull back and start guiding them. Instead, concentrate on your form and take your normal swing, and make sure to use a complete follow-through.
- When you have a chance to close out a point, never hit a more difficult shot than is necessary. Do not aim for the corner with an overhead and run the risk of hitting it out when you have half of the court to hit to, for example.

Keep Between the Lines

Most matches are won by the player who commits the fewest errors, not the one who hits the most winners. A screaming forehand down the line that barely skims over the net will draw applause from spectators, but it counts for just one point and will quickly be forgotten if you hit three consecutive backhands into the net on the next three points and lose the game.

When humanly possible, *keep the ball in play.* This may sound like simple advice, but it is surprising how many players forget to follow it, due to lack of confidence, lack of concentration, or simple fatigue. For example, do not give up on the ball your opponent hits into the corner; instead, chase it down and return it, even if your return is a weak lob. Your opponent may end up putting away the next shot 80 percent of the time, but if you do not bother to even return the first ball, she will win the point 100 percent of the time.

Keep It Deep

Unless you are playing against Jennifer Capriati, you will find that keeping your opponent at or behind the baseline with deep shots can be one of the most, if not the most, effective strategies for winning tennis. For all but the most advanced players, hitting a winner from the baseline is far more difficult than hitting one from the forecourt (the area between the service line and the net). For one, you have more time to react to a ball your opponent has hit from behind the baseline.

Also, she will find it more difficult to hit an angled shot from that position.

Hitting deep does not mean landing all of your shots within an inch of the baseline. The distance from the service line to the baseline is 18 feet; strive to have your shots land halfway between the baseline and service line or beyond. To do this, remember that the shot that clears the net by a half-inch, though impressive-looking, usually lands in the forecourt. Next time you watch a pro match, notice that most players' groundstrokes clear the net by between two feet and five feet, and land well back in the court. This gives them an advantage they can exploit.

Have a Plan, But Don't Be Afraid To Make Adjustments

Be aware of your strengths and recognize how you win points. From this, you can formulate a plan for each match. Will you play aggressive tennis, or play defensively, or try to out-steady your opponent? Only you can answer those questions by keeping track of what has worked for you in the past. Once you have a general plan of how you intend to win, recognize that you will rarely, if ever, play a match in which everything you do works as planned. This could be due to your play or to your opponent's play. Perhaps your forehand is giving you problems, or you are having difficulty adjusting to your opponent's serve. Whatever the case, at some point you will probably have to rethink what you are doing, and, if necessary, make some alterations.

These should not be wholesale changes. For example, if your opponent's kick serve is causing you headaches, you may want to stand a step or two closer to the service line so you can hit the ball on the rise. The key is to think through the problem—and always try to do this between games and not during points—and take steps to correct it, rather than letting it simmer and become a bigger issue. As for your overall match plan, do not throw it out the window if you lost the first set 7-5. Instead, focus on what has worked and what has not, and adjust accordingly.

Control the Net

If you are comfortable playing at the net, try to come in as often as possible behind your first serve. (If you are not comfortable playing at the net, practice until you are comfortable!) This will put pressure on your opponent and force her to try and pass you or hit a lob. Either way, you are dictating play.

This does not mean you have to come to the net after every successful first serve. You do not want to let your opponent get into a rhythm by coming to the net all the time. Often, if you merely make a move toward the net and make your opponent think you are coming in, she will alter her shot anyway, and you can capitalize.

First Serve In

As mentioned earlier in this book, the serve is often considered the most important shot in tennis because it starts each point and is the only shot on which you have complete control of location, spin, and pace. For those reasons, it is crucial to put your first serve in as frequently as possible. This will put pressure on your opponent, who usually will not be planning to attack your first serve, and will take pressure off you, as you will not have to worry about double-faulting.

Many recreational players make the mistake of taking a big whack at the ball on their first serve and then patty-caking their second serve. This has the effect of: a) lowering your first-serve percentage; and, b) giving your opponent an easy shot on your second serve. You do not have to hit a big first serve to be successful. Mixing up where you place your serve and what spin you use will do at least as much to put your opponent at a disadvantage.

Seize the Moment

Opportunities to take control of a point should be pounced on, particularly against a tough player. If your opponent gives you a short return to work with—one that lands inside or near the service line—you need to go on the attack. Your decision will be dictated by the location of the ball and where your opponent is on the court. If you decide to attack, you have more options because you can now angle your shot and force your opponent wide to either side, and hit an outright winner or force a weak return. Monica Seles was one of the best at gobbling up short returns and hitting balls that were at progressively sharper angles. Sometimes, by the second or third shot her opponents would be making their returns almost from the first row of the bleachers!

Drill

With both players at the baseline, your partner feeds a ball deep to your forehand, then short (inside the service court) to your forehand, then deep to your backhand, then short to your backhand. You hit each deep ball crosscourt and each short ball down the line. This will help you work on placing your groundstrokes as you build up endurance.

FROM THE BASELINE: WHEN IN DOUBT, GO CROSSCOURT

This is an old tennis saying that bears some repeating, for two main reasons: one, when you hit crosscourt, you are hitting over the middle part of the net, which is the lowest point, thus giving you a greater margin for error; two, the ball is traveling farther before your opponent returns it, which gives you more time to get back into position for her next shot. In addition, most players feel more comfortable hitting balls crosscourt because there is more court to work with.

It may seem natural to hit a shot down the line if you are pulled wide by an opponent's crosscourt shot—after all, you are hitting into

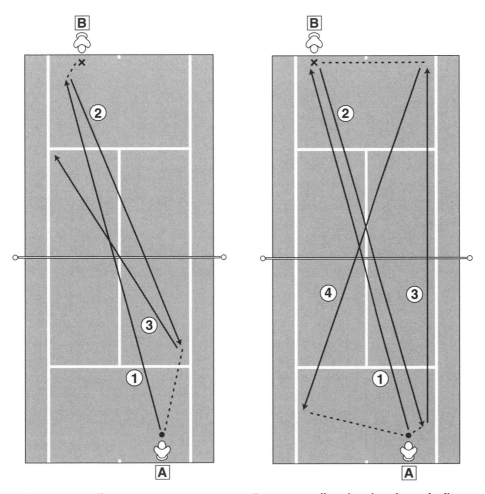

Crosscourt rally   **Crosscourt rally using shot down the line**

the open court. But this is a classic mistake made by players of all ages. Unless your shot is a clean winner or close to it, you will be even more out of position for your opponent's next shot. Instead, wait for a clear opening before you hit down the line—a short ball, for example. You can force your opponent into hitting a short ball by hitting crosscourt at a successively sharper angle.

Drill 1

Divide the court in two down the center line, with you and your partner standing diagonally opposite each other. Play points hitting exclusively crosscourt, so that your shots land on your partner's half of the court. Also, specify whether you are hitting forehands or backhands, and hit only from that side. Keep score, giving a point each time the other player hits the ball to the wrong half of the court or hits a backhand instead of a forehand (or vice versa).

Drill 2

To add a challenge to the above drill, try hitting to three areas on the crosscourt side: the deep corner, the spot where the service line meets the sideline, and a spot on the sideline between the service court and the net. This will get you used to hitting crosscourt at sharper angles. You will notice that it's more difficult to hit to the spot inside the service court when you are behind the baseline. Similarly, mark off an area with cones or other markers in the left and right corners of the court. Keep score of how many crosscourt shots you can land in the marked-off area, then switch to the other side and do the same.

AT THE NET: FIRST, GO DOWN THE LINE

This is another common mistake: volleying toward the open court too early in a point. Too many times, players hit a decent approach shot, come to the net and get a playable volley from their opponent, then hit a weak or midrange crosscourt volley into what looks like open court. Their opponent then runs down the ball and whacks a passing shot by them. Frustration sets in for the volleyer, because she did the right thing, which was to hit away from her opponent. The problem with this is that unless your opponent is far out of position or unless your volley is perfectly angled, you are exposing yourself at the net if you make the first volley crosscourt.

It is often better to hit the first volley down the line, since doing so will allow you to continue to cover the angles for a potential passing shot. Your opponent may be expecting a crosscourt volley, so you may end up wrong-footing her and winning the point. Even if you don't, you will be keeping your opponent on the defensive. On the second volley, or even the third, you can grab the opportunity when it presents itself to go crosscourt with your opponent out of position.

Exploit Her Weakness; Maximize Your Strengths, and Vice Versa

Every player you face will have a part of her game that is a weak point. It may be her second serve, or her backhand, or perhaps her overall net game. Some players have difficulty playing short balls, for instance. It may take a few points or it may take several games for you to gain this insight. You need to identify these weaknesses, and use that knowledge to your advantage. You also need to play away from her strengths whenever possible.

If she hits a soft second serve, step in and attack it. If she is struggling with her backhand, make her

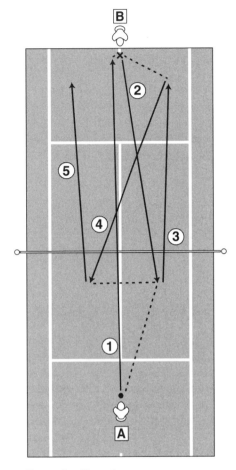

Second volley winner

keep hitting it. Of course, you must gauge if she is merely experiencing a temporary slump or whether there is an actual flaw in her game, or else you could run the risk of helping her to regain her stroke. Whenever possible, play to her weakness on big points (break points, set points, match points). If she freezes up on passing shots, even if you are an average volleyer, you may hold the advantage in these situations.

You can deal with her strengths in more than one way. If she has a big forehand, for example, you can try to hit to her backhand as much as possible . . . or you can do the opposite. Since a player's forehand often is her prime weapon, she will take more chances with it and make more errors. If you make her hit many forehands, once she makes a few errors in a row, the fact that her best shot is betraying her can be devastating psychologically.

In similar fashion, you need to play to your own strengths. Do not hold back when there is a chance to gain an advantage in a point. If you have a great crosscourt backhand, use it! If your opponent cannot handle your flat first serve, do not start messing around with spins and slices.

Do not read too much into how a player hits a ball during warmup. Some players hit a great Topspin backhand before the match starts, but do not have the confidence to hit it during play. Concentrate on what happens once the points count.

Drill

Have your partner feed you balls down the middle and approach the net down the middle. Hit your passing shot to either side to move your partner off the center line. Have her hit a return volley to you so that your next passing shot can go into the open court. This will teach you to create a passing lane when your opponent is at the net.

TAKE SOME CHANCES

When you are playing someone you have never played before, you will probably have to take a few games to get accustomed to her game, particularly her serve. Start out by playing it safe with your returns, making sure to get the ball back in play. Once you have seen enough of her serves to get a read on them—and you also have gotten into a rhythm with your strokes—take some chances and attack on your returns. This will put pressure on her early in the point.

ADJUST TO YOUR OPPONENT

Most players can be classified into a few general categories. It is up to you to identify what kind of player you are playing and figure out how you can make her do the things she does not want to do.

Attacking your opponent's serve

Baseliner

She probably does not feel comfortable coming to the net . . . which is exactly where you want to make her go. Use drop shots or short, sliced balls to the middle of the court to draw her in, then pass her or lob over her. Or, hit directly at her and make her hit volleys.

Serve-Volleyer

She is the opposite of the baseliner, so you will want to keep her away from the net. Do this by hitting your groundstrokes deep, moving her around the court, and hitting deep lobs when you are on the defensive. Try to get as many serves in as possible to keep her back.

Power Player

Players who hit the ball harder than you will eat you up if you try to play their game. Instead, change speeds on them, like a pitcher who mixes in a curveball and change-up with his fastball. Hit some short balls—hard hitters frequently will overhit the return and send it over the baseline—and use slices from both sides. Then, if she starts to slow the pace down in response, show her some of your own power.

The Pusher

Maybe the toughest opponent to beat consistently. This is the type of player who creates headaches for you by playing defensive tennis, getting every shot back, and being maddeningly consistent. Do not fall into the trap of trying to overpower her; this can lead to frustration. Hit high and deep, and alternately draw her in to the net and attack when the opportunities present themselves, such as on short balls. Above all . . . be patient! Recognize that you are going to be out on the court longer than you would against a different type of player. Focus on keeping your form and footwork consistent, and do not try to play her game.

KNOW YOUR SURFACE

Different surfaces favor different types of players. A serve-and-volleyer can look like a fish out of water on a slow clay surface, just as a baseliner who hits with heavy topspin will usually find herself at a disadvantage on grass. You can have success on the different surfaces if you adjust your game, and, perhaps more important, your mental approach. Here are some tips:

Clay

One of your toughest challenges will be to stay patient when balls you hit that would be winners on hardcourts are tracked down by your opponent and returned back to you. It is easy to get frustrated and try to hit winners to shorten the points, which usually produces bad results. Instead, tell yourself you will probably be on the court for a while, and that you need to be patient on each point and ready to strike when an opportunity arises. Use drop shots, lobs, and deep top-spin shots frequently; make your opponent work harder than you to win points. Concentrate on getting your first serve in, rather than trying for aces on the slower surface.

Grass, Indoor Carpet, Outdoor Hardcourt

These surfaces require an altogether different approach from that used on clay courts. Points will be shorter, and the serve and return become crucial. When you feel you are in a good serving rhythm, go for a big first serve and follow it to the net. You will get more free points this way. Just be sure to place your first volley so that you do not give your opponent time to set up and hit an easy winner past you. Be ready to immediately take advantage and attack, as the opportunity can come at any time during a point. Drop shots can be effective on grass, but are more difficult to control on hardcourts and should be used more as a surprise tactic.

ADJUST TO THE CONDITIONS

Bright sun or a strong wind can be used to your advantage. If you are playing in the middle of the day and the sun is high overhead, do not think twice about hitting a lob if you are in a defensive mode. Your opponent may have to let the ball bounce before hitting it, which will give you more time to recover and get into position.

If you are hitting into the wind, make an extra effort to hit your shots deep, particularly lobs, which can sometimes get blown back on your side of the net if you do not hit them deep enough. Realize that your opponent's shots are probably going to land deeper because the wind is behind her.

If you are hitting with the wind at your back, use more topspin on your shots so that they dip down and land in the backcourt. Do not hold back on your shots; on the contrary, use the wind to add pace to your shots and put your opponent at a disadvantage.

13

STRATEGIES FOR PLAYING WINNING DOUBLES

How much does doubles tennis differ from singles tennis? Tennis is tennis, you might be thinking at this point. How different could the two be? Well, think again.

While it is true that the same shots are used in singles and in doubles, that is where the similarity ends. It has been said that singles is a game of speed, while doubles is a game of finesse. In singles, you are responsible only to yourself, and your focus is zeroed in on one opponent. In doubles, on each point you must keep track of the ball, plus the position of two opponents plus your partner. In singles, you have only yourself to rely on, while in doubles you have a partner who can bail you out when you make a mistake—but who also is relying on you to do the same.

Positioning and court coverage are crucial to winning at doubles, as are teamwork and communication. The latter can take time to develop, which is why you could take two superior singles players and pair them together, and they would probably lose to a good doubles team that had been playing together for a while. Great singles players may not necessarily make great doubles players, and vice versa, but playing doubles will definitely improve your overall tennis skills by forcing you to react more quickly, refine your volleying technique, and be more accurate on your returns and groundstrokes.

POSITIONING

There are three basic formations for playing doubles: Both-Up, Both-Back, and One-Up, One Back. The last one is the most common position to use when starting a point, while the first two usually are dictated by what happens during a point.

Both-Up Formation

This is actually the most ideal position to be in, since more often than not it means you are controlling the point. Since you obviously cannot start a point in this position—one of you has to serve or return serve, after all—you have to move into this position during the point.

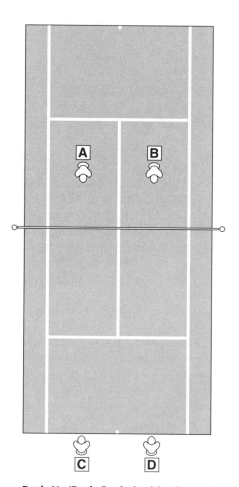

Both-Up/Both-Back doubles formation

Many elite doubles teams strive to play Both-Up almost all the time, which is a style that is also called *attacking doubles.* It is an offensive position that requires that both of you have strong, reliable volleys and overheads, since you will most likely be hitting one or the other. For young or beginning players, it is wise to wait for an opportunity—but when one comes, do not hesitate to both come to the net.

Advantage: You put your opponents on the defensive, and force them to attempt a lob or passing shot; you cut down your opponents' angles and options.

Disadvantage: You are susceptible to a well-placed lob; you risk having your opponents use you for target practice if you hit a weak or short volley.

Both-Back Formation

While the Both-Up formation is a purely offensive position, the Both-Back position is

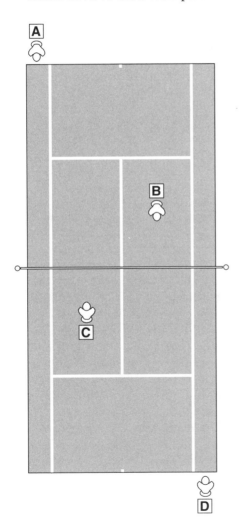

almost strictly a defensive position. It is used out of necessity, usually when an opponent's shot has pushed you or your partner out of position and forced you to hit a lob.

You should try to avoid being in the Both-Back formation in all situations except when your opponents are in the Both-Up formation. When this happens, for example, when you have hit a short lob, you will be surprised how often you can stay in the point by staying at the baseline. The key is staying patient and letting your opponents make the mistake.

Advantages: You and your partner cover the baseline so your opponents have to hit a well-placed overhead to win the point.

Disadvantages: You are not in a good position to play an angled shot or drop shot; it may take a concerted effort to get back to the net and regain control of the point.

One-Up, One-Back Formation

This is the most common doubles formation and is used by doubles teams at all ability levels. Unlike the offensive (Both-Up) and defensive (Both-Back) formations described above, the One-Up, One-Back formation is a combination offensive-defensive formation. The net player plays an offensive role, cutting off opponents' shots before they reach the backcourt, and the backcourt player covers the baseline and guards against lobs.

Advantages: You have coverage of the forecourt and backcourt; the net player can poach or switch sides during a point to throw off an opponent's timing.

Disadvantages: A diagonal gap between the front and

Up-and-Back doubles formation

back player that can be exploited by the opposing net player. This is sometimes called *The Hole.*

One-Up, One-Back: Offensive and Defensive Positioning

When you and your partner are playing One-Up, One-Back, the one who is playing at the net will often move into a defensive position to shrink the gap between you and make it more difficult for your opponent at the net to volley the ball down the middle. This can be done by dropping back so that you are standing about on the service line. This puts you in a better position to play a shot toward the hole. It is important to remember not to drop back too far, or you will end up in no-man's land and will be out of position to hit a clean return.

Two customary situations in which to use defensive positioning are if your opponent at the net has a play on the ball, or if your partner is having trouble returning your opponent's first serve. In both cases, there is a good chance that your opponent will have an opportunity to volley the ball between you and your partner.

In the offensive position, you remain in a normal volleying position, about eight feet from the net. This will widen the gap between you and your partner, but will put you in a better position to close in on balls hit by your opponents and volley them for winners. You should be in this position whenever the opponent in the backcourt is playing the ball. If you get a chance to hit a volley, your best percentage shot is to go down the middle, between your two opponents.

Switching

When you use the standard One-Up, One-Back formation, there will be many instances when you and your partner will have to switch sides. Depending on the situation, either you or your partner needs to call out "Switch!" so that there is no confusion—or else you will end up losing the point and probably looking pretty silly too. Switches most often occur when:

- Your opponent hits a lob over you at the net;
- You poach at the net and your momentum carries you well over onto your partner's side, and;
- The opposing net player poaches and crosses the center line.

There will be other times when you need to switch, depending on the position of you and your partner, and the placement of your opponent's shot. Some doubles teams like to use what is called the Australian doubles formation when they are serving. In this alignment, the net player on the serving team lines up on the same side as the server (or sometimes, positions herself right in the center and ducks down below the net to avoid being hit by the serve). This keeps the player returning serve guessing, since you have the option of staying on your side while your partner shifts over to cover the open court, or moving over yourself.

TIPS ON PLAYING WINNING DOUBLES

Remember—It's "Doubles"

Doubles is a team sport, and the interaction and communication between you and your teammate/partner may be the single most important factor in playing good doubles. While it is a given that each player brings different physical skills to the court, it is each player's personality and mental makeup—and how those traits mesh with those of her partner—that can hold the key to a successful partnership.

A good starting point is to remember that you and your partner win and lose as a team, regardless of who played better or worse in a particular match. There will be points in every match where you make up for your partner's errors and vice versa. The scoreboard does not reflect which of you is the stronger player, only how many points and games you have won together.

Here are some key points to remember when playing doubles:

- Accept your partner's abilities—strengths *and* weaknesses—and work toward capitalizing on the former and protecting the latter.
- If your partner is more skilled than you, swallow your pride and concentrate on exploiting your strengths and improving your weak areas.
- Be positive. This sounds obvious, but it is extremely important, particularly when things are not going your way in a match. Use an error by your partner as an opportunity for encouragement.
- Gauge your partner's moods and tendencies and know when you need to offer verbal support or just stay out of her way. This can take a little time to develop, but the rewards will be worth it.
- Avoid being negative. If your partner is playing poorly, using criticism or sarcasm as a motivational tool will probably only make her play worse.
- Communicate! Silence is not golden on the doubles court. Good doubles teams check in with each other between most points to discuss strategy for the next point or share an observation about

an opponent's weakness. Even if you just touch rackets or nod to your partner and say, "Let's get 'em this time," you are reinforcing the bond between you. Questions or problems should be verbalized before they start affecting your play as a team.

Poaching: If At First You Don't Succeed . . .

Poaching, in which the player at net moves toward the middle of the court to cut off the opponent's return before it reaches the backcourt, should be a staple of any doubles strategy. It puts pressure on your opponents, often results in outright winners, and, at the very least, makes them adjust their thinking.

When should you poach? It depends on the opponent, the situation, and your partner, but a good rule of thumb is to do it as soon as you have the opportunity rather than wait, since you may not get another chance in that point. Here are some other general rules on poaching:

- Make the decision to poach *before* your opponent hits her shot. Base your decision on the strength and placement of your partner's shot. A shot by your partner down the middle is better to poach on because your opponent is more likely to hit the ball back at a favorable angle, compared with a wide shot which creates an opportunity for your opponent to hit an angled shot you cannot reach.
- When poaching on a service return, make sure your partner knows you are going to do it so that she can hit her serve down the middle. Some doubles teams use hand signals to communicate this; others do it verbally between points. You and your partner can agree on this beforehand.
- Watch your opponents closely and try to pick up their tendencies. Does one of them telegraph her down-the-line shots by standing a certain way when returning serve? These little observations will help you anticipate better.
- Time your move for when your opponent starts to swing her racket forward, as she will have already committed to where she is going to hit the ball.
- Move toward the net instead of laterally when you are poaching. You will reach the ball sooner and be in a better position to hit a strong volley.

Above all, do not abandon the strategy if you miss a few chances. Keep poaching! If your opponents see you have packed it in, they will gain confidence. At the 2001 U.S. Open, Chandra Rubin and partner Els Callens were on the verge of upsetting Venus and Serena Williams when Rubin hit weak half-volleys on two separate points that were pounded past her for winners. Rather than becoming tentative, however, Rubin continued to play aggressively, and it was her lunging forehand volley winner—the result of a well-timed poach—that set up Callens's service winner on match point that completed the upset victory.

The Serve

In doubles, serving accuracy is far more important than serving the occasional ace and relying on your second serve the rest of the time. Your goal should be to get your first serve in most of the time, and to hit both your first and second serve with spin. The reason for this is twofold: by taking some pace off your serve and adding spin, your accuracy will improve; and, you will have more time to come to the net to play your opponent's return.

It is a good rule to remember to serve down the middle, which will have the dual effect of reducing the angles for the receiver and giving your partner at the net a better chance at poaching the return. Be sure to keep your opponents off balance by mixing in wide serves, but make sure to communicate this to your partner, as she will have to guard against a return down the line.

Whoever is the stronger server of you and your partner should serve the first game.

Returning Serve

In doubles, the return of serve is probably the most important shot in any point, mainly because there is the added obstacle of your opponent playing at

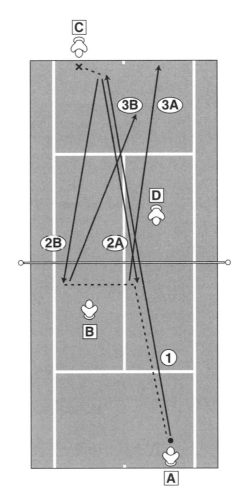

Doubles rally: serve down the middle

the net. Making a solid return becomes a psychological as much as physical challenge with her lurking there, waiting to pounce on your return and hit a volley winner. But there are several general rules to remember when returning serve in doubles that will help you stay in the point:

- The crosscourt shot is the standard (and safest) return to make, since you are bypassing the player at net and getting the ball into the backcourt. Try and angle your return so that the server has to go wide; landing it near the outside corner of the service court will also make her move forward and, more often than not, produce a high return that can be volleyed easily.
- Shorten your backswing if need be, and go for controlled, accurate shots rather than looping shots produced by a long backswing.
- Hitting with topspin will make your shots drop and make them more difficult for your opponents to volley with authority. Even a shot that barely lands over the net will cause problems if it has topspin and dips below the level of the net, causing a volley that is angled upward.
- Do not worry about "running around" your backhand to hit a forehand return if, say, your forehand is your stronger shot. Remember, your partner is there to cover the rest of the court if you are slightly out of position. Making a return that puts pressure on your opponents is the primary goal.
- The opposing net player knows that you will try and go down the line at some point, but only you know when. If the opening is there, go for it, even if you went down the line on the previous shot. Otherwise, pick your spots. Or, hit your return directly at her; chances are she will be moving laterally to the left or right, and may be caught off-balance.
- If your opponent is an aggressive serve-and-volleyer, mix in a few lobs on your returns to force her to retreat back to the baseline. This is particularly effective if either opponent is having difficulty hitting overheads.
- Do not try to hit outright winners on service returns, as there is rarely enough room on the court to do this anyway. Instead, concentrate on placing the ball and mixing up your shots so that you keep your opponents guessing.

Controlling the Net

It is a tennis truism that the doubles team that controls the net will usually win the point. To do this, you need to have the attitude that you are both going to come to net as soon as an opportunity presents itself. This could be as a result of a strong first serve by you or your partner; a weak second serve by your opponent; a short groundstroke return by your opponent, or a strong groundstroke by you or your partner that puts your opponents at a disadvantage.

If you and your partner are both at the net, your opponents will have to either try to pass you, usually with a shot down the middle or down the line, or hit a lob over you. You must be prepared for all the scenarios.

Remember that it is much harder to hit a winner on your first volley in doubles than it is in singles. The general rule is to hit your first volley down the middle. If your opponents are playing One-Up and One-Back, this will frequently produce an outright winner between them. If they are both at the baseline, a shot down the middle will cut down the angles for a potential passing shot.

If you and your opponents are both at the net, try to aim your volley downward, toward their feet. This will force a return that pops up in the air which you can put away easily. The next best thing is to hit the ball at your opponent's body (without trying to hurt anyone), particularly at her hip on the racket side. This is the most awkward volley for her to make, and will usually result in a weak return.

Drill 1

Start with both doubles teams at the baseline. One player feeds the ball to start the play, and the point becomes live after the ball crosses the net twice. The goal is to win the point, ultimately, which means attacking the net. You should look for opportunities (a short ball or floating ball) where you and your partner can both move up. This will help you develop both offensive and defensive strategies, as both teams are starting in a neutral position. Keep score, with the first team to reach seven points winning the game. Switch partners after the first game or two.

Drill 2

This drill places a premium on attacking the net and closing out the point. All four players start from just outside the service line. Team 1 feeds the ball to Team 2, and the point begins as soon as Team 2 makes contact with the ball. Both teams usually end up at the net, which makes for some fast action. Work on angling your volleys to win the point. Play to 11 and switch partners if you choose.

"Yours" or "Mine"?

There will be frequent occasions when you and your partner are both in position to hit the ball. If this occurs, it helps to have agreed on some general rules beforehand to avoid hesitation when you have a split second to make a decision.

For example, some players believe that the person who hit the last shot should be the one to play the return, since she may already be anticipating where the return is going to go. A basic approach is to agree that the stronger player will take any 50-50 shots, or that whoever is in position to hit a forehand (if that is her stronger side) should take it. Whatever the case, it is worth hashing this out ahead of time to avoid confusion.

Defending Against Lobs

There is not much you can do if one of your opponents hits a lob that lands on the baseline. Most lobs, however, will land closer to the net and should be played aggressively to finish the point. Do not wait for the ball to bounce, as it will give your opponents more time to recover and get in position—unless, for example, it is windy and you want to ensure you get an accurate swipe at the ball.

If you are playing at the net and the lob is going to land between the net and the service line, it is your ball, and you should play it while your partner keeps her position. If the lob is deep and you will not be able to reach it, recognize this immediately and communicate it to your partner. When she retrieves it, you should switch sides to cover the side of the court she just left. If you are both at net you should both retreat to play the deep lob, and try to work your way back to the net as soon as possible.

Anticipation

If teamwork is one of the most important pieces of the doubles puzzle, anticipation is not far behind. While you will not always be able to know where the ball is going on every shot, staying aware and alert on the court will enable you to get in position to make your best return. This is particularly important when you are playing at the net, when split-second reactions frequently are required. To do this, you have to watch not only the ball, but also be aware of where your partner is and where your opponents are on the court. All of these will come into play on an average point.

One way to make this second nature is to keep your eyes focused on your opponents at all times, and not on your partner. This may sound simple, but it takes a little practice. When you are playing at the net, practice focusing solely on whichever opponent is playing the ball. As your partner hits the ball past you, focus first on your opponent at the net. If the ball goes into the backcourt, shift your focus to

Doubles: watching your partner (incorrect—keep your eyes on the opponent)

the opponent in the backcourt. Watch each opponent's preparation, swing, and contact closely. This will give you a sense of what each player likes to do in different situations.

Some examples of anticipation:

- You are playing net in the deuce court and your partner hits a forehand down the line. The opposing net player will have a clear path for her volley down the middle of the court, so you move to your right to cut off the opening. It is surprising how many players forget to do this.
- Your partner hits a big first serve down the middle. You move to the middle to poach the weak return.
- Your opponent hits a lob that your partner has to retrieve at the baseline. You move back to the baseline along with your partner so that your side of the court is covered if your opponents hit an overhead.
- Your partner hits a lob into the ad court, over the player at the net. You notice your opponent in the backcourt focusing on the ball and not on where you are, and when she hits a looping return toward your partner's side—which she assumes is open court—you move over and smash it for a winner.

Good anticipation also is the product of watching your opponents' tendencies. What do they like to do in certain situations? Once you catch them on it, they may be more crafty next time. But you have succeeded in making them alter their play, which means you are gaining an edge.

More Tips

- Unless both opponents are playing at the baseline and you are in a favorable position, save your drop shots for when you play singles. Remember that drop shots usually are less effective when you are playing on hardcourts.
- Avoid hitting half-volleys as much as possible by moving in to the net more quickly. Getting caught in no-man's land is a sure-fire way to lose a point.
- Hit your overheads aggressively. Holding back on them or hitting them tentatively will let your opponents get back into the point.
- There is no dishonor in hitting lobs. They keep your opponents off-balance and can often turn the tables in a rally.
- When both opponents are at the net, mix up your shots. Go down the middle, down the line, hit a few lobs, maybe even dink the ball a few times. Do not get predictable; make them wonder what you are going to do.

DOUBLES RULES

Scoring is the same in doubles as it is in singles, but there are other unique rules that must be followed:

The Court

The entire court area is considered in play, including the 4½-foot *doubles alleys* on either side. The player serving can stand anywhere between the center mark (the short line perpendicular to the baseline that divides the baseline into two halves) and the point where the sideline and baseline intersect.

Serving and Receiving

Players toss a coin or spin a racket to determine which team will serve first, and then decide on the serving order. The team that won the toss decides which partner will serve first, and the opposing pair chooses who will serve the second game. The partner of the player who served in the first game shall serve in the third; the partner of the player who served in the second game shall serve in the fourth, and so on in the same order for the rest of the match. Changeovers occur after odd-numbered games.

The order of receiving the serve will be decided at the beginning of each set as follows:

- The team receiving the serve in the first game decides which partner will receive the first serve, and that partner will continue to receive the first serve in every odd game for the rest of that set.
- The opposing team decides which partner will receive the first serve in the second game, and that partner will continue to receive the first serve in every even game for the rest of that set. Partners receive the serve alternately throughout each game.

According to United States Tennis Association rules, if your partner is receiving the serve, you are allowed to stand in any position on your side of the net, on or off the court. However, if a serve that is not a *let* (one that hits the net and falls on the other side of the court) touches the receiver's partner or her racket before it hits the ground, the server wins the point. Any serve that touches either the server's partner or her racket before it hits the ground is considered a fault.

If a player serves out of turn, the correct player should serve as soon as the mistake is discovered. All points scored, and any faults served before the discovery of the error, will count. If a game is completed before the discovery is made, the order of serve remains as altered. If the receiving team alters its order by mistake, the game is played out and the players go back to the original order in the next game in which they receive serve.

The Ball in Play

In the course of making a return, only one member of a doubles team may hit the ball. If both of them hit the ball, either simultaneously or consecutively, it is an illegal return. A return is not illegal if players' rackets touch other while one of them hits the ball.

14

TENNIS PSYCHOLOGY— THE INNER GAME

"(Insert name of sport) is 90 percent mental." Athletes, coaches, and commentators are fond of applying this saying to just about every sport imaginable, and there is a measure of truth to the high numbers. Your mental state dictates your physical actions and reactions, and thus has a direct effect on your performance. With apologies to baseball, football, and the rest, tennis may be the most "mental" of the major sports, since it is largely played one-against-one, with no team framework to provide support or encouragement.

Each tennis match actually consists of three submatches. One is mostly physical, while the other two are mental. They are, in ascending order of importance:

- You against the ball and the court. This takes into account how you actually hit the ball, whether your mechanics are correct, how you react to put yourself in the best position to return the ball, and how you place your shots. Your physical conditioning and practice habits are revealed here.
- You against your opponent. This is the *mano-a-mano* aspect of tennis: how you respond to the unique challenges posed by each individual player, how you counter her shots, and how you exploit her weaknesses.
- You against yourself. This is probably the most important aspect of any tennis match. For everyone from beginning players to experienced professionals, keeping a positive mental attitude

and handling the little failures and frustrations that are part of every match can be more difficult than handling a tough opponent. When players of more or less equal ability play against each other, whoever wins this submatch usually wins the overall match.

It takes a positive attitude and a certain amount of self-confidence just to step out on a tennis court; after all, you could be like a lot of people and just stay home on your couch watching TV. But even though playing competitive sports guarantees that at some point you will experience failure and frustration—sometimes over and over during a match!—the rewards are well worth it. The question is, how do you build and harness that self-confidence so that it translates into peak performance?

This is a major issue for even some of the top players in the world. It may look as though an Andre Agassi or Venus Williams is effortlessly going about his or her business during a crucial part of a match; in reality, it is their years of developing a positive mental outlook that makes it look so easy. These are players who, when they get behind love-30 in a game, do not say to themselves between points, "Uh-oh, if I lose two more points I'll lose this game, and I'll fall behind in the set." Instead, they say, "OK, I know I'm going to win this game, it's only a question of how I'm going to do it." Even if it doesn't always come to pass, they know they have given it their best shot by not beating themselves.

This section will offer advice on developing and maintaining the type of mental attitude that can keep you performing at your peak. It is important to remember that this is a gradual process and will not happen overnight. But with consistent, regular effort, you may begin to see some improvement fairly quickly.

VISUALIZATION

Visualization is a technique that has become increasingly popular with elite and professional athletes over the last several years. It is based on the idea that our brains process something we have vividly imagined in much the same way they process something that actually happened. In other words, if you vividly imagine yourself serving strongly and accurately in your next match—including imagining the feel of the service motion and the sound of the racket hitting the ball—then your brain and nervous system will treat it as though it has actually happened, which will make you better prepared to turn the vision into reality.

This is not to say that you should stop practicing your serve. On the contrary, visualization will only work if you combine it with your regular workouts. But many athletes have found that they can more accurately recreate the physical conditions of a match in their mind than they could during a typical practice session.

How Do I Do It?

To start with, you need to remember that visualization is something that will take practice to develop. You may also need to adjust your physical surroundings to create a relaxed environment in which there are no distractions. You can do this anywhere, as long as you can put yourself in a calm, relaxed state so that you are able to clear your mind of any outside thoughts and you can concentrate on visualizing.

There are two methods used in visualization. You can envision doing the motions yourself, so that you are experiencing the sensations firsthand. This is called Subjective Visualization. Or, you can "watch" yourself in the second person, which is called Objective Visualization. This is like watching a videotape of yourself. Subjective Visualization is effective at working on the physical skills you will need in a match, while Objective Visualization may help you more with intangibles such as how you will react in certain situations.

Some guidelines to follow when you are visualizing:

- Practice your visualization regularly; try to spend some time on it each day, no matter if it is only five or 10 minutes. The important thing is to be consistent.
- Be detailed with your visualizations, and use all your senses. This will enhance the effects of the images.
- In addition to envisioning yourself hitting volleys, serves, and groundstrokes, envision yourself reacting calmly and in control during a stressful situation during the match; for instance, when one of your shots is called out when it was clearly in.
- Pinpoint any specific skills or shots that have been giving you trouble—hitting an overhead, for example—and visualize practicing these skills. This will help you when you are actually on the court practicing.
- If you have access to video images of yourself playing, use these to aid your visualization.

STAYING MOTIVATED

In tennis, as in life, it is not always easy to maintain your enthusiasm for what you are doing. You may feel that your game is not improving at the rate you would like it to, or that you are not winning the matches you feel you should be winning. At these times, it is easy to question whether all the effort you are putting in is worth it.

Because it is such a demanding sport, tennis has more than its share of stories about young pros, in particular female players, who have become burned out from playing and, in some cases, drop off the circuit altogether. The most famous of these is Jennifer Capriati, who cracked the top 10 in the early 1990s while still in her midteens but left the women's tour for more than two years before returning and winning the 2001 Australian and French Opens. Sadly, Capriati's turnaround is the exception rather than the rule when it comes to cases of tennis burnout.

It does not matter whether you compete at a high level or play for recreation; motivation is the driving force behind any forward strides you make as a player. It helps you deal with frustration, tackle difficult situations, maintain a practice routine, and handle pressure.

Why do tennis players lose motivation? There are many causes. If you are a young player, it can be related to pressures you put on yourself or pressures that come from your parents or coaches. For older players, it can stem from diminishing returns in the form of losses or a leveling-off of skills. A common thread in many cases is a sense that playing tennis is not fulfilling psychological needs, whether these are for personal growth, monetary gain, approval from others, or simply for recognition.

Defining Success and Setting Goals

Success is the solution to most motivation problems. This sounds surprisingly simple, but there is more to it than meets the eye. It all comes down to how you *define* success, and making sure your definition is a realistic one that won't set the bar too high or too low. In sports and in society in general, "second place is for losers" unfortunately seems to have become the prevailing idea. If you don't "win the big one," people seem to say, it does not matter that you won all the matches or games to reach "the big one" while all the other players or teams except one have been eliminated. This is ridiculous, of course, unless you are one of the top players in the world and expect to win most tournaments. The rest of us need to measure success in terms other than just wins and losses, though naturally those will factor into the equation.

Try not to view success as just another word for winning. It should instead be tied in with giving your best effort, improving your game, mastering a new stroke, or any number of other things. For example, say you are trying to develop an all-court game that features strong groundstrokes mixed in with regular net approaches. But you do not yet feel confident enough to commit to playing this way, so during matches you revert to dinking your opponents to death, and wind up winning some of the time using this strategy. What is wrong with this picture? In effect, you are winning the battles but losing the war—the war being the higher level of tennis you aspire to play.

Achieving success as you progress as a tennis player requires setting goals for yourself. These are basically challenges you make to yourself, and they can be big or small, short-term or long-term. They can be as modest as learning to put a new spin on your second serve, or as ambitious as earning a scholarship to play tennis in college, or even playing on the professional circuit. The key is to understand the relationship between performance goals, which focus on things like improving your game, and outcome goals, which focus on the end result—wins and losses, rankings, and so on.

"Outcome goals are not necessarily in your control, whereas performance goals are things you control on a daily basis," according to Paul Lubbers Ph.D., Administrator of Coaching Education for USTA Player Development. "Staying on track with your performance goals—like going out on the court and giving 100 percent effort every day in practice, or hitting a certain number of serves every day, or staying focused on your game style—will then lead to outcomes. If you are focused solely on outcome, you are creating a whole source of problems regarding on-court performance, because you are setting yourself up for failure. You become outcome-oriented, and therefore you set yourself up for choking and all the things that go along with that."

Following are some examples of short-term, midterm, and long-term goals you might set for yourself. Whether these apply to you will depend on your age and ability level. Note that the short- and midterm goals are performance goals, while the long-term goals are more outcome-based. Try to make your short-term and midterm goals realistic. If they are too ambitious, you will be setting yourself up for repeated failure and frustration. If they are too modest, you will be shortchanging yourself.

Short-term

- Improve my physical conditioning by performing daily strength and flexibility exercises.
- Work hard in practice so that I make the most of my practice time and develop consistency in my strokes.
- Plan what I eat and drink so that I can perform at my peak during practice and matches.

- Seek advice from my coach or instructor about weaknesses in my game.

Midterm

- Diversify my game by adding a new shot or a new strategy; for example, develop a net game or add a slice backhand to my repertoire.
- Improve my existing strokes and correct any flaws.
- Use visualization techniques to improve my concentration and mental attitude.
- Play well against players whose styles have given me trouble, e.g., play more patiently against players who are pushers.

Long-term (Outcome Goals)

- Attain a high junior ranking in my section.
- Make my high school's varsity team.
- Play No. 1 singles for my varsity team.
- Win a state or sectional singles title.
- Earn a college tennis scholarship.
- Play professional tennis.

KEEPING FOCUSED

Anyone who has played or watched tennis has witnessed this scenario played out many times: a player is cruising along in a match, when suddenly things start to fall apart. It could be a bad line call, or a few unforced errors in a row. Whatever the case, the player starts to lose her composure and begins loudly criticizing herself after each mistake. She may slam the ball into the net in frustration, or throw her racket. As she continues to unravel emotionally, she starts trying to hit winners on every shot, which only brings more frustration as the errors mount.

The average two-set tennis match consists of more than 100 points, which means that unless you are playing someone who is far inferior to you, you will probably lose at least 40 percent of the points even if you end up winning the match. In other words, if you agonize over every point you lose, you will end up wasting a lot of time and energy and severely limit your chances of being successful. You need to be able to forget what happened 10 seconds ago and focus on what you are going to do in the next 10 seconds. Likewise, when you reach a critical point in a match—a break point, set point, or match point, for instance—you need to be able to approach it in as calm and as confident a manner as possible so that your mind and body are prepared but not overprepared.

Often, this is much easier said than done. Even the best players in the world experience frustration when they are not playing their best. What separates them from the rest, however, is their ability to process and channel that frustration so that it ceases to become a negative force, and often turns into a positive force. Part of their secret lies in routines, according to Lubbers.

"It's important to have well-established routines between points, before points, between games, where you're able to slow down," he said. "The best players in the world utilize routines that enable them to walk to the baseline, whether it is to serve or return, with a clear head and a clear mind, and focus on performance, not outcome."

How can you handle frustration or adversity when it comes your way in a match? Here are some tips:

- Slow down! This means your breathing, your actions . . . everything. Take a few extra seconds to collect yourself before you hit your next serve or get into position to return your opponent's serve.
- Relax your muscles between points. Dissipate some of the tension by relaxing your shoulders and neck and shaking out your arms and hands.
- Forget about what happened on the last point or what you hope will happen two games from now. Focus on what you have to do right now, on this point. Seven-time Wimbledon champion Steffi Graf was so good at doing this that once in a while, she would lose track of the score in a game because she was so focused on playing the next point.
- Center your thoughts on what you have to do, not on what your opponent is or is not doing.
- Try to focus your thoughts away from the negative and towards the positive. Instead of replaying in your mind how you have lost the last three points on unforced backhand errors, visualize yourself hitting a solid backhand into the corner.
- Take a mental step back and enjoy yourself a little bit. Don't stop trying your hardest, but remember that this is not a life-and-death struggle; you are playing a tennis match, which is supposed to be fun.

Sometimes, extraordinary circumstances will make it more difficult for you to maintain concentration during a match. These may have to do with outside factors unrelated to tennis. For example, imagine you had to play your younger sister in the final of the U.S. Open. That's exactly what Venus Williams faced in September 2001, and she found herself worrying too much about Serena's game and not enough about her own . . . until, as she later explained, she was forced to regain her focus:

"It was kind of like if I was sitting in the stands and Serena was playing someone else and I was saying, 'Come on, Serena, just do this or do that,'" Venus Williams said. "When I'd find myself doing that, I'd lose a couple of points. When I lost a couple of points, I wasn't sorry anymore."

Tip: Make your practices as much like matches as possible, especially if you are adding a new stroke to your repertoire. Try to simulate match conditions by playing tiebreak sets, full-length sets, or other games in which you keep score (see Chapter 18 Games). Use the same mental approach you would use in a match. This will get you used to handling pressure.

BREAKING A SLUMP

For the last several weeks you have been hitting the ball well, cutting down on unforced errors, and winning matches with regularity, sometimes even with ease. Then suddenly, for no apparent reason, your forehand starts to betray you, your serve ceases to become a weapon, and your volleys are landing six inches out instead of six inches in. You are now experiencing that dreaded athletic malady, the slump. Slumps often seem to come out of nowhere, and often disappear for no discernible reason. Fortunately, there are several identifiable factors that can cause slumps and efficient strategies for combating them.

Causes

- Change in physical skills: Learning a new shot or a new technique often causes a drop in your level of play as you absorb the change. There usually is an in-between period as the new method gradually replaces the old. If possible, it may be helpful to introduce these changes during periods when you are not actively competing.
- Natural learning plateaus: You have reached a certain skill level and do not appear to be progressing any farther. This is inevitable when you are mastering complex physical skills, a process that does not seem to follow any set pattern.

- Physical changes: You may be going through a low period physically, due to an injury or other malady that is affecting your play; or, you may not be eating right or getting enough sleep.
- Mental changes: Low self-confidence, negative attitudes, or simply the pressures and tensions of day-to-day living can manifest themselves in performance slumps.
- Increased awareness: When you are more keenly aware of physical and mental changes, you may have difficulty putting them aside and letting your natural instincts and athleticism take over.

Solutions

- Understand and accept that your slump is a result of your current physical and mental state, and make a commitment to reevaluate those aspects.
- Talk to someone—your coach, instructor, teammate, or parent. They will be able to give you an objective opinion on what may be causing your drop in play.
- Take a break from your training schedule. Often you will find that even a day or two away from the routine helps you approach things with a new attitude.
- Focus on what is fun. Revisit your goals and objectives and remind yourself why you enjoy playing.
- Stay in top physical shape, and even increase your fitness level. This will keep you sharp mentally and physically, and will help you maintain your level of play late in matches.
- Spend 10 to 15 minutes a day visualizing yourself breaking out of your slump and reaching new levels. Reprogram your thoughts and focus on the positives (how far you have already progressed as a player, for example) instead of the negatives (your current slump).
- Allow for nature to take its course, so to speak. Realize that you cannot force changes to happen, but that they will happen naturally when the surrounding factors are right for them to happen.

Few players are more qualified to talk about slumps than Gabriela Sabatini. The 1990 U.S. Open champion who was once ranked No. 3 in the world, Sabatini went from winning five tournaments in 1992 to winning none for the next two and a half years. During the long drought there were many frustrating losses, but she persevered and eventually triumphed at the 1994 Virginia Slims end-of-the-year championships, beating Martina Navratilova and Lindsay Davenport, among others. After beating Davenport for the title, Sabatini spoke about the ingredients needed for playing winning tennis.

"There are a lot of things that have to be there," she said. "You have to feel good about your tennis and how you're hitting the ball. If you can have that confidence, then you can be focused. But the confidence comes from feeling good about yourself, feeling good about hitting the ball, feeling good physically. Then you're able to give it all."

MATCH PREPARATION

Talent can go a long way, but talent without mental preparation is like a racket with a hole in the middle. Too often we see players who possess the strokes and athleticism but not the mental strength to bring it all together, and thus never reach their full potential. For this reason, your preparation for a match can be critical to your actual performance.

There are as many ways to prepare as there are players. Some players need to be nervous to get psyched up; some do not. Some players need to be alone with their thoughts; some need to be around people. Lubbers remembers a story about Olympic skiing gold medalist Picabo Street, who habitually seemed to be running late, often making it to the starting gate just in time for her run. What unsuspecting bystanders did not know was that this was all part of the plan. "She needed the adrenaline rush to get a boost," Lubbers recounted.

Create your own prematch preparation routine, based on what feels comfortable. If it works, stick with it. Here are some general do's and don't's:

- Keep your normal training routine, including eating, sleeping, and practicing. Don't make significant changes to what has worked for you in the past. Too much practicing could burn you out; too little could make you lose your competitive edge.
- Spend time each day visualizing how you want to perform in general and how you want to react in specific situations. Don't wait until the night before, or you may become obsessed.
- Be mentally and physically prepared for anything you might encounter in the match; recognize the possibilities, both good and bad, and think of how you will respond. Don't try to make changes in your physical skills or techniques at the last minute, since this can be disruptive.
- Avoid feelings or situations that may have negative effects on your preparation. Try to be emotionally upbeat. Don't involve

yourself in activities that could leave you feeling depressed or sad; this can lead to a flat, uninspired performance.

- Use nervous energy to your advantage. It is perfectly normal to be anxious before an important event . . . as long as you don't make it worse by becoming anxious about being anxious! Accept being a little nervous, and tell yourself it means that you are psyched up.
- Do whatever it takes to create a winning atmosphere. If this means wearing a lucky article of clothing or following a prematch ritual, go for it. Don't change your routine—for example, do not eat several protein bars right before your match—just because of the importance of the match.
- Commit yourself to giving 100 percent, staying positive, and having fun. If you do this, you cannot lose no matter what the final score.

Drill

Sit down with a pencil and piece of paper, and remember the last time you played really well. Then write down what you did leading up to the match—from the day before to right before you stepped onto the court. Include what you ate, how much you slept, what you thought about, what stretches you did, what you did during warmup. Repeat the exercise for when you did not play well. You will probably notice some obvious differences.

"Playing well is not random," Lubbers said. "It is about routines."

JANA NOVOTNA

Imagine the most devastating defeat you have ever experienced. It may have come to a friend, or to a high school opponent, or at a junior tournament. Now, imagine it happened on Wimbledon's Centre Court, tennis' most hallowed ground, with millions of people watching your personal ordeal on television.

What you have imagined is what happened to Jana Novotna in 1993. Perennially one of the women's tour's top singles players and an accomplished doubles player, Novotna lacked the one ingredient that would put her in the elite class of players— a Grand Slam singles title. She seemed poised to put her name in the record books at Wimbledon in 1993 when she beat, among others, Gabriela Sabatini and Martina Navratilova to reach the final. Playing on Centre Court against Steffi Graf, Novotna found herself serving in the third set, one point away from a 5-1 lead.

Suddenly, her game betrayed her. She double-faulted on game point and had her serve broken by Graf, and went on to lose the next four games and the match. During the trophy ceremony, Novotna broke down in tears and was consoled by England's Duchess of Kent in a scene that was replayed countless times on television stations all over the world.

No one likes to lose, but losing is a fact of life that all players have to get used to. Still, this was a particularly tough defeat to swallow. Each time she played at a major event, Novotna would be asked about the Wimbledon loss. But Novotna had become one of the best players in the world by keeping a relentlessly positive attitude, and she refused to start doubting herself or her abilities. Instead of answering questions about the defeat, she would politely steer the topic back to what she was doing currently. And she learned from the experience and resolved not to let it happen again.

The result was that Novotna's play became more consistent, and she eventually rose to a career-high No. 2 in the world. Along the way, she won the end-of-the-year women's championships in 1997, and followed that by returning to Wimbledon in 1998 and winning on the same court where she had experienced such frustration five years earlier. It was a fitting reward for a player who would not allow herself to dwell on the negative.

"It's really important to always believe in yourself and to have a dream," Novotna said after winning Wimbledon. "But you have to go out and work every day, do a lot of planning, and keep on working from one year to another. This is what I have been waiting and working for."

15
INJURY PREVENTION

Sports commentators are fond of saying that "injuries are part of the game," and to a great extent they are correct. Everyone who plays sports regularly and plays them hard will eventually come down with some type of injury, be it a jammed finger or a broken leg. Tennis in particular, with its unforgiving playing surfaces, quick starts and stops, and unpredictable changes of direction, makes players of all levels susceptible to potentially debilitating injuries.

The trick is to take all the necessary steps to prepare yourself so that your muscles and joints can withstand the rigors of playing tennis, so that you spend as little time as possible on the sidelines. This means more than just hitting a few practice shots before a match. It means warming up and stretching your muscles before you play, and cooling down after you have finished.

WARMUP

The first building block to any injury prevention strategy is to make sure you are warmed up and ready to play before you toss up the first ball. Though this sounds simple enough, many players forget to do it, and many end up with sore muscles, or worse, as a result.

Your warmup can be as brief as five or 10 minutes, and will help you achieve the following:

- Increase blood flow to your muscles.
- Raise the temperature of muscles and tissue.
- Speed up your heart rate, which prepares your cardiovascular system for exercise.

- Decrease muscular tension.
- Speed up your nerve impulses, which enables you to move more efficiently.

Just about any kind of low-intensity aerobic activity will do the trick. This could mean walking, light jogging, stationary biking (if you have a bike handy), or light hitting on the court. The idea is to ease into a light sweat without pushing yourself. That will come later, during your practice session or match. Many professional players like to start their workout by jumping rope, which uses the arms and legs and works up a sweat quickly.

STRETCHING

Once you are warmed up, it is time to perform stretching exercises to further prepare your muscles and joints for the stresses of playing. Warming up before stretching—rather than in the reverse order—is important because you will be able to stretch more efficiently when the blood is flowing to your muscles.

There are many different types of stretches (see Chapter 16) that address the different muscles in your body, but there are some general hints that apply to all stretches that will help you get the most out of stretching:

- Try not to tense your muscles while you are stretching. Relax your muscles and go slowly; take this time to think about what you are trying to accomplish in your practice or match.
- Hold each stretch for a minimum of 15 seconds, with a goal of eventually holding it for 30 seconds to a minute.
- Do not bounce while you are stretching; make each motion slow and deliberate.

COOLING DOWN

Cooling down after you exercise can be nearly as important as your warmup and stretching. It is especially important for tennis players, who often play grueling matches in hot weather, and need to avoid muscle cramps when they get off the court.

After you have finished playing, take a few minutes and stretch out the muscles you focused on during your preworkout stretching. This will help prevent those muscles from becoming sore over the next 24 hours. Also, try not to stay in a sitting position for too long after a strenuous workout. Walk around a little bit; this will keep the blood from pooling in your legs, and will help prevent muscle cramps.

If you feel that you have suffered an injury, you should seek medical advice immediately rather than trying to make a self-diagnosis. Your physician will be able to pinpoint the problem and suggest an appropriate course of action.

AVOIDING HEAT ILLNESS

All tennis players, even experienced professionals, are susceptible to the effects of extreme heat and the stresses it can put on your body. If you are like most people and you play most of your tennis outdoors during the summer, you need to know the right precautions to take and the right warning signs to watch for in order to safeguard yourself against heat illness.

Your body is like a car engine—when it is not cooled properly, it can overheat and break down. This can manifest itself in the form of muscle cramps, heat exhaustion, or, in extreme cases, heat stroke.

Muscle cramps caused by dehydration usually affect your leg muscles or abdominal muscles, and occur when there is not enough blood flow to these muscles. The muscles' balance of water and electrolytes (salt) is disrupted, causing the muscles to tighten up.

Heat exhaustion is also a product of dehydration, and can cause dizziness, chills, headache, and nausea. You may also experience a rapid pulse, heavy sweating, or elevated temperature.

Heat stroke is a medical emergency and can be fatal if not addressed immediately by trained professionals. Symptoms are similar to heat exhaustion, but can progress to more serious symptoms such as disorientation, body temperature of more than 104 degrees, irregular heartbeat, loss of consciousness, or seizure. A crucial warning sign that you may be headed toward heat stroke, and one that is frequently misinterpreted, is when you stop sweating. This is a danger sign that urgent medical assistance is necessary.

How to Protect Yourself

The most important thing to do when you are playing on a hot, humid day is to drink plenty of fluids. You cannot rely on your body's thirst-feedback mechanism to know how much to drink, so you need to drink at regular intervals—about every 15 minutes—even if you do not necessarily feel thirsty. You need to drink about a quart of fluid for every pound of body fluid you lose during exercise. Also, remember that humidity will cause you to sweat a lot even if the temperature is not soaring.

Here are some other tips:

- Try to plan your activities early in the morning or late in the afternoon to avoid exposure during the hottest hours of the day.
- Know your limits, and know when to say "no" to exercise. Overdoing it is not a good idea in any weather, but in hot weather it can be dangerous.
- Avoid caffeine and alcohol before and after you are exercising, since they cause you to lose extra fluids.
- Wear a hat or sun visor to protect you from the effects of direct sunlight. Try to find one that is made of light, breathable material like cotton.
- Wear loose-fitting clothing made of light fabric, like cotton, and wear light colors instead of dark, as they will not absorb as much sunlight.
- In addition to drinking fluids, pouring cool water over your head can promote heat loss.

Treating Heat Illness

Heat illness is nothing to take lightly. If you are playing in hot weather and you have moved beyond general fatigue to the point where you are experiencing some of the symptoms listed above, stop immediately, and get out of the sun. If you are suffering from muscle cramps, try stretching and massaging the affected muscles, then ice them for 15 minutes. Drink plenty of fluids, preferably at room temperature instead of ice-cold, as your body will absorb these faster.

If you believe you are suffering from heat exhaustion, you should seek assistance from an onsite doctor or trainer, or call for one immediately. In the meantime, retreat to a cool place and remove any excess clothing and apply cool water to your body, either directly or with a wet towel or sponge. Drink as much fluid as you can.

Heat stroke is a medical emergency, and should be treated by trained medical professionals. Immediate treatments include ice packs near large arteries such as at the neck or armpits, and oral or intravenous replenishment of fluids.

TENNIS ELBOW

Tennis elbow, or lateral epicondylitis, is one of the most common tennis injuries. It affects the tendon that attaches a group of forearm muscles to the elbow, and is usually caused by repeated stress on the hand and wrist. Many nontennis players who perform repetitive motions with their hands and wrists are at risk for developing tennis elbow.

While tennis elbow does not sound like a particularly serious injury, it can sideline you for months if you ignore the warning signs and try to play through the pain. If you are experiencing elbow pain that persists for more than a day, or that recurs when you play, discontinue playing for a few weeks. You can use ice and nonprescription anti-inflammatories (aspirin, ibuprofen) to relieve discomfort, but you may need to consult a physician if symptoms continue.

Preventing Tennis Elbow

Tennis elbow often is caused by incorrect stroke mechanics. In other words, the way you hit the ball may be causing the pain in your elbow. Therefore, you can decrease your chances of suffering from tennis elbow by refining your stroke with the help of a tennis instructor or club pro.

Here are some tips to remember:

- Hitting the ball with excessive topspin puts stress on your wrist, forearm, and elbow. Try to moderate the amount of topspin you use, and mix up your shots (which is a good idea anyway!) so that you are not hitting every shot the same way.
- Keep all the parts of your swing coordinated. This means being in the Ready position, using correct footwork and anticipation, and swinging through the ball with a smooth, fluid motion.
- Hitting the ball with your arm straightened can transfer too much of the shock of the ball's impact to your elbow. When hitting forehands, keep your arm slightly bent even as you make contact with the ball—this will allow your upper arm and shoulder to absorb some of the force of the swing. When serving, try to keep your arm slightly bent and try to avoid having your wrist and hand locked into a rigid position.
- On backhands, you can lessen the vibration absorbed by your arm by making sure not to put your thumb behind the racket grip. In all strokes, your swing should involve your whole body— legs, hips, lower and upper arm, and shoulder—so that no one part has to carry too much of the load.

If you are returning to play after suffering from tennis elbow, it is crucial to remember not to try to do too much, too fast.

Start slowly and increase the length and intensity of your practice sessions gradually. This will help ensure that your joints and muscles get used to the specific stresses caused by hitting a tennis ball.

Consult a teaching pro about your stroke. He or she will probably be able to analyze any faults or hitches in your swing mechanics, and suggest ways to remedy them. You may also be using the wrong type of racket for your size or ability level, which may be contributing to your arm problems.

Conditioning

Following are some examples of stretching and strengthening exercises for the wrist and elbow that can help reduce your chances of getting tennis elbow. All stretches should be done using a gentle, fluid motion, and should be held for at least 20 to 30 seconds. Always check with your physician or physical therapist before beginning any stretching and strengthening routine.

Stretching

STRETCHING ARMS I
Hold one arm straight in front of you, with the wrist flexed and the fingers pointing up. Grasp the hand and thumb with the other hand, and pull the wrist down. Hold for 10 to 15 seconds. Repeat 10 to 20 times.

Next, flex the wrist and point the fingers down. Grasp the back of the hand and the thumb with the other hand, and pull the wrist down. Hold for 10 to 15 seconds. Repeat 10 to 20 times.

STRETCHING ARMS II
Standing, straighten your arm out in front of you. Flex the wrist and point the fingers down, until you feel a stretch across the top of the forearm. Next, flex the wrist and point the fingers up, until you feel a stretch across the bottom of the forearm.

Stretching Arms I: pulling fingers with off hand

Stretching Arms II: hand pointed down

Stretching Arms III: hand pointed up

Elbow flexion: start

Elbow flexion: finish

Strengthening

The following exercises should be performed three to five times a week, using two- or three-pound weights. Start off by doing 10 repetitions, and when you can do this with ease, increase to two, then three sets of ten. Increase the weight by a pound or two, and drop back to two sets until you feel comfortable enough to go back to three.

ELBOW FLEXION
Stand with your arm at your side, palm facing your body. Bend your elbow, while rotating your palm to face upward, lifting the weight slowly. Keep your upper arm steady. Return to the starting position and repeat.

ELBOW EXTENSION
Lie on your back with your elbow pointed toward the ceiling. Your elbow should be bent so that the weight is held next to your head, palm facing inward. Place the opposite hand on the triceps for support. Extend your elbow completely, until your arm is straight. Keep your upper arm steady. Return slowly to the starting position and repeat.

FOREARM SUPINATION
To perform this exercise, take the weight off one side of the bar and use a bar weighted at only one end. Sit with your forearm supported on a table or on your thigh, so that your hand can move freely. With your palm facing down, hold the unweighted side of the bar with your thumb facing the weighted side. Rotate your forearm until the bar and your thumb are pointed at the ceiling, keeping your elbow as still as possible. Return slowly to the starting position and repeat.

Elbow extension: start

FOREARM PRONATION
To perform this exercise, take the weight off one side of the bar and use a bar weighted at only one end. Sit with your forearm supported on a table

Elbow extension: finish

Forearm supination: start

Forearm supination: finish

Forearm pronation: start

Forearm pronation: finish

so that your hand can move freely. With your palm facing up, hold the unweighted side of the bar with your thumb facing the weighted side. Rotate your forearm until the bar and your thumb are pointed toward the ceiling. Hold your upper arm and elbow as still as possible. Return slowly to the starting position and repeat.

16
CONDITIONING

No matter what sport you play, there is no substitute for being in good physical shape—especially in a sport like tennis, where conditioning often can be the difference between winning and losing. Being in good shape can help you get through a tough third set, but it can also help your overall game, by improving your quickness, agility, strength, and mental concentration.

General conditioning is as important to your game as your serve and groundstrokes. This means getting in shape before you step onto the tennis court. You may hear some players say they are going to "play themselves into shape." Aside from taking the easy way out, this approach usually leads to early-season injuries, as a player's muscles and joints may not yet be ready for the rigors of competitive play.

You need to start with a sound base. One way to achieve that is to include the four basic types of exercise in your physical conditioning routine. They are as follows:

Aerobic training includes any activities that get your heart working at a higher rate than normal for an extended period. Aerobic exercising—jogging, biking, swimming, even brisk walking—strengthens your heart and makes it more efficient, improves your ability to use oxygen, and burns fat and calories. Even if you do not lose weight—muscle weighs more than fat, after all—you will move better and tire less easily on the tennis court.

You should strive to engage in some type of aerobic exercise at least three times a week, for a minimum of 20 minutes. Start slowly, and increase your activity level gradually. Find something you enjoy doing and you will make the effort to fit it into your schedule.

Achieving *flexibility* is the best way to prevent injury and soreness. You should do stretching exercises before and after each workout. (See below for some examples.) Staying loose and flexible will not only keep you out of the doctor's office, but also will help you when you are lunging for a volley at the net or reaching up for an overhead.

Strengthening exercises burn fewer calories than an aerobic workout, but they provide other benefits. Building more muscles increases the rate at which you burn calories, as muscle requires more calories than fat. Strengthening exercises usually involve weights, and there is a wide variety of weight-training programs. For tennis players, key muscle groups to focus on include the shoulders and back, hips (adductors/abductors), hamstrings, and calves.

In general, it is best to start with light weights that you can lift 12 to 15 times without tiring. Gradually increase the weight, keeping the same number of repetitions. Consult a coach or trainer for advice on starting a program tailored to your needs.

Anaerobic exercises involve short bursts of activity at a high level of energy. Sprinting and weightlifting fall under this category, as well as any other activity (biking or swimming) that incorporates intervals of increased rate or intensity. This will help when you need to get off the mark quickly when you are running down a drop shot.

There is an infinite variety of ways to get in shape, and you should let your creativity take over. If jogging is not your cup of tea, try a stairclimbing machine or elliptical trainer at your local gym. If you are not keen on biking, use a rowing machine (or get out on the water and do it for real), or go cross-country skiing. The key is to vary your activities so that you do not get in a rut, and you improve your aerobic and anaerobic fitness, strength, and flexibility. This is called cross-training, and it has immense benefits for all athletes, particularly those who play a demanding sport like tennis.

The world's top players understand this, and incorporate variety into their workouts. For example, Venus and Serena Williams often throw a football the length of the court to simulate the service motion, or play soccer on the court to improve their footwork. Amanda Coetzer performs exercises with a medicine ball to strengthen her shoulders, and does interval training—alternating sprinting with walking or jogging—to work on explosive starts and stops. Lindsay Davenport combines jumping rope, running uphill, stationary biking, and light weightlifting, while Mary Pierce adds quick bursts (30 seconds at maximum intensity) using a treadmill, abdominal crunches, and a stairclimber, before finishing a workout with swimming laps.

OVERTRAINING OR OVERPLAYING

Exercising builds up your body's strength, but it also depletes your energy supplies. This goes for playing tennis too. If you are spending too much time pushing your body without giving it time to rest and recover, you may be overtraining, which can lead to injuries and illness.

Sometimes you are so focused on getting in shape or maintaining your edge that you may not notice that you are overtraining. Here are some telltale signs:

- Overall fatigue that occurs whether you are exercising or resting
- Feeling irritable or anxious, or depressed
- A decrease in appetite
- Unnatural weight loss
- Persistent muscle or joint soreness, or nagging injuries
- Difficulty sleeping
- Nausea or stomachaches
- Frequent colds or minor ailments.

The best solution is to rest. Even a couple of days off can make a significant difference, and studies have shown that even a week off will have a marginal effect on endurance and a negligible effect on strength. When you resume, make sure to stay hydrated and eat properly (see Nutrition in Chapter 16), and vary your exercise routine as described above.

STRETCHING AND STRENGTHENING EXERCISES

Following are some examples of specific stretching and strengthening exercises. If you have questions about which exercises are right for you, consult your coach, personal trainer, or physical therapist. Particularly if you are recovering from an injury, it is important to get professional advice on how to proceed, so that you do not aggravate an existing injury.

When performing any stretching or strengthening exercise, remember to use a smooth, fluid motion, as jerky or sudden movements can cause injury. Stretches should generally be held for a minimum of 15 seconds to get the full benefit. You should eventually be able to hold a stretch for 30 seconds to a minute.

Stretching: Head and Neck

CHIN CIRCLES
Reach your chin forward. With your chin, draw a circle down and around, ending with your chin tucked back toward your throat. Repeat five times. Reverse the direction of the circle, and repeat five times.

HEAD ROTATION TO THE SIDE

Slowly turn your head to one side. Hold the stretch for a count of three. Slowly return to the starting position. Then turn your head to the other side. Hold the stretch for a count of three. Return to the starting position. Repeat five to 10 times. Try doing a set two or three times a day.

HORIZONTAL NECK TILT

Slowly tilt your head to the side. Stop when you feel a strain, but be careful not to go so far that your ear touches your shoulder. Hold the stretch for a count of three. Slowly tilt

Head rotation to side

your head back to the starting position. Then tilt your head to the other side. Hold the stretch for a count of three. Return to the starting position. Repeat five to 10 times. Try doing a set two or three times a day.

VERTICAL NECK TILT

Slowly tilt your head back until you can look up at the ceiling. Hold the stretch for a count of three. Then slowly tilt your head back to the

Vertical neck tilt I

Vertical neck tilt II

starting position. Lower your head until you can look down at the floor. Hold the stretch for a count of three. Return to the starting position. Repeat five to 10 times. Try doing a set two or three times a day.

Stretching: Arms, Shoulders, and Wrists

ARM STRETCH
With your right hand, grasp your left elbow in front of you. Look over your left shoulder, and pull your left elbow toward your right shoulder. Hold for 15 counts. Repeat two or three times, and do the other side.

FLEXING WRISTS
With your fingers extended, flex your wrist and stretch fingers up to the ceiling and down to the floor. Repeat 10 to 20 times.

RAISED ARMS
Stand straight and raise your arms straight above your head. Lace your fingers together, palms facing up. Push your arms back and up, until you feel the stretch in your arms, shoulders, and back. Hold for 10 to 15 seconds. Repeat four to six times.

ROTATING WRISTS
Make a fist, and rotate your hand from the wrist. Do this in one direction 10 times, and in the other direction 10 times. Next, open your fist, and rotate your hand with the fingers extended.

SHOULDER BLADE CRUNCH
Lace your fingers together behind your head. Move your elbows back to pinch your shoulder blades together. Hold for three counts and relax. Repeat three times.

SHOULDER BLADE STRETCH
While standing or sitting, reach around your chest and try to grasp your shoulder blades with your opposite hands. Drop your chin toward your chest. Inhale and hold onto your shoulder blades for a count of 15. You should feel the stretch along the border of your shoulder blades.

Raised arms

Shoulder blade stretch: front

Shoulder blade stretch: back

SHOULDER AND UPPER ARM STRETCH

For the right shoulder: Standing, grasp the back of your left shoulder with your right hand. Hold your right elbow in your left hand, and gently pull the elbow to the left, until you feel a nice stretch. Reverse directions for the left shoulder.

STRETCHING ARMS

Standing, straighten your arm out in front of you. Flex the wrist and point the fingers down until you feel a stretch across the top of the forearm. Next, flex the wrist and point the fingers up, until you feel a stretch across the bottom of the forearm.

WRIST EXTENSOR STRETCH

While standing or sitting, raise your arm 80 degrees, keeping your elbow straight and palm down. Using your opposite hand, bend the hand down so your fingers are pointing toward the floor. You should feel the stretch in your wrist and the outside group of forearm muscles.

WRIST FLEXOR AND ELBOW EXTENSOR STRETCH

Standing or sitting, raise your arm 80 degrees, keeping your elbow straight and palm up. Using the opposite hand, bend the hand down so your fingers are pointing toward the floor. You should feel the stretch in the tendons of the wrist and the inside group of the forearm muscles.

Stretching: Back and Chest

BACK AND ARMS STRETCH 1
Standing, link your hands together behind your back. Rotate your elbows inward while you straighten your arms.

BACK AND ARMS STRETCH 2
Standing, link your hands together behind your back. Lift your arms up until you feel a nice stretch. Hold for 10 to 20 seconds. Repeat, as you like.

BACK AND ARMS STRETCH 3
Standing, reach your arms behind at shoulder level, and grasp something like both sides of a doorway. Lean forward and straighten your arms. Hold for 10 seconds. Repeat, as you like.

Back and arm stretch

BENDING SIDE-TO-SIDE
Stand with your arms by your sides. Bend from the waist toward one side and then the other. Repeat up to 50 times.

LOWER BACK STRETCH
Lie on the floor and relax your back muscles. Slowly bring your knees up to your chest. Curl your arm around your knees. Hold for 15 to 20 seconds. Repeat 10 times. You can also do this exercise raising one leg at a time.

Stretching: Legs

HAMSTRING STRETCH 1
Lie on your back with one leg straight in front of you and the other bent. Hold onto the ankle of your bent leg and slowly straighten your leg. Keep your lower back on the floor. Hold for

Lower back stretch

Hamstring stretch: both legs

Hamstring stretch: single-leg

10 seconds. Relax. Repeat five to 10 times.

HAMSTRING STRETCH 2

Lie on your back. Lean forward to grasp the outside of your ankle. Pull the leg toward your chest. Hold for 15 to 30 seconds. Repeat four to five times.

HAMSTRING STRETCH 3

Sit on an exercise table (or a reasonable substitute), with one leg off and one leg straight in front of you. Keeping your back straight, reach forward with outstretched arms. Hold for 15 to 30 seconds. Repeat six to 10 times.

QUADRICEPS STRETCH 1

Lie on your side, resting the side of your head in your hand. Stretch your bottom leg out on the floor. Hold the foot of your top leg, and pull the heel toward the buttock. Hold for 10 to 20 seconds. Repeat four to five times.

QUADRICEPS STRETCH 2

Sit with one leg bent, touching the heel of the foot to the hip. You can bend the other leg as well, or leave it straight in front of you. Hold for 10 to 20 seconds. Repeat four to five times.

QUADRICEPS STRETCH 3

In a sitting position on the floor, straighten your legs as much as possible. Keep your back straight and lean slowly forward until you feel a stretch. Hold for 10 to 20 seconds. Repeat four to five times.

Stretching: Knee, Ankle, and Foot

ACHILLES AND ANKLE STRETCH

Start in a kneeling position. Lift one knee so the toes are even with the knee of the other leg. Lift the heel of the bent leg, until it is elevated about a half-inch. While you lower the heel, lean forward on your thigh. Hold 10 to 20 seconds. Repeat five to 10 times.

CALF ACHILLES TENDON STRETCH 1

Stand arm's length from a wall, and lean forward on your hands. Move one foot forward, and one foot back a bit. Keep the heel of the back foot flat on the floor. Stretch forward until you feel the stretch in the back of the knee. Hold for 10 seconds. Unlock the back knee and bend it toward the wall, until you feel the stretch in the lower leg, closer to the heel. Hold for 10 seconds. Repeat eight to 10 times.

ACHILLES TENDON STRETCH 2

Kneel on the floor. Inhale as you shift one foot slightly forward. Keep the foot flat, with the bottom of the foot facing up. Exhale and lean forward. Hold that stretch and relax. You will feel the stretch in the top of the foot. Repeat 10 times.

Calf Achilles stretch: start

ANKLE AND CALF STRETCH

Sit back in a chair, with your feet flat on the floor. Keeping your heels on the floor, lean forward in the chair. If necessary, push your knees down. Hold for 45 seconds. Repeat five to 10 times.

ANKLE CIRCLES

Sit on the floor or in a chair. Remove shoes and socks. Moving only your ankle, draw circles. Repeat 10 to 20 times.

STRENGTHENING

The following exercises are designed to strengthen the muscles and joints you use

Calf Achilles stretch: finish

Abdominal crunch

when you are playing tennis. Consult with your trainer or coach if you have questions about which exercises may not be right for you.

Strengthening: Back and Abdominal

ABDOMINAL CRUNCH 1
Lie on the floor, with your knees bent. Cross your arms on your chest, and use your stomach muscles to curl your head and shoulders toward your thighs. Hold for only a few seconds. Repeat 15 to 20 times.

ABDOMINAL CRUNCH 2
Lie on the floor, with your knees bent. Place your hands under your hips, and use your stomach muscles to bring one knee up to your chest. Hold for five to 10 seconds. Repeat 10 to 20 times.

LEG LIFT
Lie on the floor, with one leg straight in front of you and the other bent. Slowly raise your straightened leg as far as you can. Hold for 10 seconds. Repeat five to 10 times.

PELVIC TILT
Lie on the floor, with your knees bent. Slowly tighten your stomach and buttocks as you press your lower back onto the floor. Hold for 10 seconds. Repeat five to 10 times. You can also lift your pelvis a bit while you are tightening your stomach and buttocks, slowly rolling from your hipbone to your lower back.

Strengthening: Arms, Elbows, Wrists, and Hands

WRIST CURLS 1
Sit in a chair, with your arm resting on a table and your hand over the table edge. Hold a one- to four-pound weight in your hand, and slowly raise and lower it by flexing your wrist. Repeat 15 to 20 times, to make one set. Perform two or three sets alternating palm up and palm down.

WRIST CURLS 2
Lie face down on a support, such as a bench. Place your head on a towel, and grasp a two- to five-pound weight in each hand. With your thumbs

up and your elbows straight, raise your arms outward and upward, then lower them. With your thumbs down, stretch your hands out from your body, until you feel your shoulder blades pinching together.

SQUEEZING BALL
Hold a soft, foam ball in your hand, with palm upward. Squeeze the ball 15 to 20 times.

TRICEPS CURL
Stand with one arm above your head holding a two- to five-pound weight. Support the extended arm with the opposite hand. Bend the elbow of the extended arm in back of you, as far as possible, and then straighten it to full extension. Repeat four sets of 15 repetitions.

TRICEPS EXTENSION
Standing, bend forward and rest one arm on a support, such as a table. With a two- to five-pound weight in the other hand, stretch the arm in back of you, perpendicular to the floor. Straighten the elbow, until the arm is parallel to the floor. Hold for five to 10 seconds. Repeat 15 to 20 times.

Triceps curl: start   **Triceps curl: finish**

Strengthening: Leg and Knee

ABDUCTOR RAISE
Lie on your side, propped on one elbow. The leg on the floor is bent. The other leg is straight. Slowly, lift the leg, hold it up for five seconds, lower it. (Using light ankle weights increases the effectiveness.) Repeat 20 to 30 times.

HAMSTRING CURL
Stand with your thighs against a surface (like facing a table or a wall). Bend one knee, as far as it can go, and hold for 10 seconds. Lower the foot slowly. (Using ankle weights increases the effectiveness.) Repeat 20 to 30 times.

Abductor raise: start

Abductor raise: finish

RUBBER BAND KNEE STRENGTHENING

Lean against the wall with your back straight and your legs extended at a 90-degree angle to your back. Wrap a rubber exercise band around your foot at the ankle and then try to extend your knee against the resistance of the rubber band. Hold for 30 seconds. Repeat exercise 10 times. Do three sets of 10, then repeat exercise with other leg.

SQUATS

Stand with your feet aligned under your shoulders and arms straight out. Keep your heels on the floor and your knees over your feet, and squat. Repeat 20 to 30 times.

STEP-UPS

Stand in front of a structure about two feet high (like a bench or a double step). Step up onto the support, straighten your knees fully, and then step down. Do this at a steady pace. Add weights to your hands, as you feel comfortable.

STRAIGHT LEG RAISES

Bend one knee and place foot flat on bed. Keeping the other knee straight, lift the straight leg up about 12 to 20 inches. Count to five slowly while lowering leg. Three- to five-pound ankle weights can be added.

Step-up: start

Step-up: finish

Prone hip extension

Strengthening: Hip and Groin

PRONE HIP EXTENSION
Lie face down on a flat, firm surface. Raise your leg from the hip, then slowly lower it. Raise your leg to a count of four, and lower to a count of eight. Do three sets of 10, then repeat with other leg.

STANDING RUBBER BAND FLEXION AND ABDUCTION
Tie a rubber exercise band around a fixed object like a banister. Wrap the band around one of your ankles. Flex the leg from the hip against the resistance of the rubber band. Extend your leg to a count of four, and flex it to a count of eight. Do three sets of 10.

STANDING RUBBER BAND HIP EXTENSION
Tie a rubber exercise band around a fixed object like a banister. Wrap the band around your ankle. Extend and lower your leg from the hip against the resistance of the rubber band. Extend your leg to a count of four, and flex it to a count of eight. Do three sets of 10, then repeat with the other leg.

Strengthening: Ankle and Foot

STRETCH CORD—EXERSION
Use a piece of stretch cord that's roughly four feet long. Place the knot outside a door, and close the door securely. Sit on a chair and cross one leg on top of the other. Put the end of the cord around the ball of the

foot on the crossed leg. Position yourself so that the cord has moderate tension.

Cross the opposite leg over. Place the cord on the outside of the foot. Rotate your foot outward. You want to feel moderate resistance. Hold for 10 to 15 seconds. Repeat 10 to 15 times.

STRETCH CORD—EXTENSION

Use a piece of stretch cord that's roughly four feet long. Place the knot outside a door, and close the door securely. Sit on a chair and cross one leg on top of the other. Put the end of the cord around the ball of the foot on the crossed leg. Position yourself so that the cord has moderate tension.

Position your chair straight back. Place the cord over the top of one foot, and extend your ankle back, towards your head, against the resistance. Hold for 10 to 15 seconds. Repeat 10 to 15 times.

STRETCH CORD—INVERSION

Use a piece of stretch cord that's roughly four feet long. Place the knot outside a door, and close the door securely. Sit on a chair and cross one leg on top of the other. Put the end of the cord around the ball of the foot on the crossed leg. Position yourself so that the cord has moderate tension.

The cord is around the ball of the foot on the crossed leg. Rotate your foot inward, so the cord is pulled tighter. You want to feel moderate resistance. Hold for 10 to 15 seconds. Repeat 10 to 15 times.

TOE RAISES

Stand with the balls of your feet and your toes on a thick book (like a phone book). Hold onto a support. Lower your heels to the floor slowly. Raise yourself slowly as far as you can. Hold for 8 to 10 seconds. Repeat 15 to 20 times.

Toe raise: start　　　　　　　　　　　**Toe raise: finish**

LINDSAY DAVENPORT

In a sport that is filled with more than its share of oversized egos, Lindsay Davenport is like a breath of fresh air. Unpretentious, thoughtful, and well-spoken, Davenport is proof that it is not necessary to be arrogant or conceited to be a world-class tennis player. Much of this undoubtedly comes from her upbringing, which was as normal as just about any other teenager's. Her parents, though both accomplished athletes in their own right, did not place undue pressure on her to become a professional player. Unlike most pros, she attended high school and graduated with her class. It was this sense of balance that gave Davenport a more rounded perspective on tennis and life.

Three years into her professional career, however, Davenport might have wanted to trade some of that perspective for a couple of major tournament titles. Like many players she had reached a plateau; her skills had gotten her to a certain level, but she was unable to advance to the next rung on the ladder. For all the power Davenport could generate on the court, she still found herself falling short against the top players. She was viewed as a "nice" player who would hold her seeding—advance to the quarterfinals or semifinals of a tournament, say—but would not be considered a serious contender. To change that would take a concerted effort both on and off the court.

The first order of business was to shed some unwanted pounds. It was a grueling process for the 6-foot-3 Davenport, who had always been big-boned. With the help of coach Robert Van't Hof, she lost 30 pounds and gained new mobility on the court. Her results began to reflect the changes, which in turn raised her confidence level. By 1996 she had her first breakthrough when she defeated Steffi Graf to win at Indian Wells, and she reached the semifinals at the U.S. Open in 1997. She then realized her lifelong dream of winning a Grand Slam title when she won the U.S. Open in 1998, and followed that by winning Wimbledon in 1999 and the Australian Open in 2000. It was fitting that Davenport defeated Martina Hingis to win the U.S. Open by running down a drop shot on match point and smacking a winner into the open court.

Lindsay Davenport has become one of the most feared players in the game. But her success has not gone to her head, in part because she does not take it for granted.

"I never thought I'd be No. 1," Davenport said in 1998 after reaching the top spot. "I always watched Martina (Navratilova), Chris, Steffi, and Monica with a different kind of respect. I idolized them all. I thought I'd have a successful career, and I wanted to win a Grand Slam, but I didn't necessarily think I could."

17
NUTRITION

THE BASICS

We have all heard it said enough times that eating right is one of the keys to good health. If you play a physically demanding sport such as tennis, it is especially important to eat the right foods, in the right amounts, at the right times, so that your body is well prepared for the rigors of competition. How do you do this? Start by remembering these three words: variety, balance, and moderation.

You need variety in your diet so that you are not consuming too much of some nutrients or too little of others. Your diet should include grains (bread, pasta, cereals), fruits and vegetables, dairy products (milk, cheese) and foods that provide protein (poultry, fish, meat and others). These foods supply you with the more than 40 nutrients your body needs to function at its peak. Of course, you will not be able to consume all those nutrients each day, so your day-to-day diet needs to be balanced so that it provides you with the necessary nutrients.

Moderation means controlling the amount of food you eat. You do not have to deny yourself your favorite foods, but you need to make sure you do not overdo it. Here are some tips:

- Keep your portions modest in size. If you have a huge plateful of food, you will be more tempted to finish it off.
- Make sure to eat at regular times, and avoid eating too much between meals.
- Avoid skipping meals, which can lead to overeating when you finally do eat.
- Be particularly vigilant about fried foods, butter, rich sauces, red meat, and other foods that may be high in fat or cholesterol. Instead of reaching for one of these foods when you want a snack, have a piece of fresh fruit or a vegetable.

Water is crucial for athletes, and this section will address the importance of staying hydrated. But you should also drink several glasses of water a day even if you are not competing, as water keeps your organs working efficiently and helps to flush the toxins out of your system.

NUTRITION FOR ATHLETES

What you eat, and how much you eat, will have an effect on your performance. There is no question about this. Your goal should be to pattern your eating habits so that you are enhancing your performance rather than detracting from it.

To understand how the diet affects performance, it is necessary to understand how the body uses food as fuel. In basic terms, the body converts simple carbohydrates, like candy, juice, or fruit, and complex carbohydrates, like pasta, potatoes, or cereal, into glucose, which your body burns for quick energy. Any carbohydrates that are not burned up are stored in your muscles as glycogen. When you are exerting yourself for more than an hour—say, during a typical tennis match—a diet that is high in simple carbohydrates will not be enough to sustain you. Your body will burn up all the glucose, leaving you feeling weak. Therefore, you need to have complex carbohydrates in your diet to provide the energy for extended activity.

Calories

Maintaining a proper body weight takes into account your age, height, and body type. It also requires being mindful of how many calories are in the foods you are eating. Many athletes focus on the number of grams of carbohydrates or protein they are getting, when they should also focus on the number of calories. As discussed above, limiting your portion sizes is an easy way of limiting your caloric intake.

Fats and Protein

All young adults need protein in their diet to generate muscle tissue. For athletes, it is not wise to follow diets that focus almost exclusively on protein, as carbohydrates and fats are equally integral to a balanced diet. Fats, which supply a source of energy for extended physical activity, must play a part in an athlete's diet. It is much better to get your daily fat intake from foods that are high in protein, such as meat or chicken, than from junk foods.

Fluids

Every athlete knows she must drink fluids when practicing or competing, especially if the weather is hot. But it may come as a surprise that you can be dehydrated *before* you even step onto the court if you have not been drinking fluids throughout the day before your match or practice. You should drink fluids about one hour before you are going to play, and at least every 15 minutes while you are playing. Do not wait until you feel thirsty before you take a drink! If you are thirsty, you are already on your way to being dehydrated.

It is equally important to drink fluids when you have finished playing. You may have lost a pound or more from sweating; if you have, Michael Bergeron, Ph.D., a member of the U.S. Tennis Association Sport Science Committee, recommends drinking fluids equal to 150 percent of the deficit—which means that if you have lost a pound from sweating, you should drink 24 ounces.

Overhydrating yourself can cause problems too. Drinking too much water, combined with heavy sweating, can produce a sodium deficit and lead to fatigue, nausea, and headache. You can avoid this by adding some salt to your diet before and after you play. According to Dr. Bergeron, good sources of salt include salted pretzels, many types of soups, cheese, tomato sauce or tomato juice, or some sports drinks.

You should never drink caffeine or alcohol before or after playing, as these are diuretics and will cause, rather than prevent, dehydration.

PUTTING IT INTO PRACTICE

If you are a serious athlete who exercises strenuously five to seven days a week, you should strive for a daily diet that consists of the following ratios (to calculate your weight in kilograms, divide your body weight in pounds by 2.2):

- Carbohydrates: 6 to 8 grams per kilogram of body weight, or about 50 to 70 percent of total calories.
- Protein: 1.6 to 2.4 grams per kilogram, or about 15 to 20 percent of total calories.
- Fat: 20 to 30 percent of total calories, and no less than 20 grams per day.

This means a 150-pound athlete's diet should include approximately 409 grams of carbohydrates and 109 grams of protein. Since most protein is high in fat and low in fiber, caution should be used when following a high-protein diet. High-protein diets can cause dehydration and, in extreme cases, kidney disease.

It is important to remember that athletes can require about twice as much protein as sedentary adults. If you exercise regularly, say, three days a week, you should follow the guidelines set forth in the USDA's Food Guide Pyramid. (http://www.ptponline.com/detail.cfm?page=183)

The following foods are good sources of protein:

- Meat, chicken, and fish: about 7 grams per ounce.
- Dairy products: about 8 to 9 grams per cup.
- Beans and legumes: about 6 to 8 grams per half cup.

Fat is a necessary nutrient in the body, but a high-fat diet will increase your risk of heart disease. An athlete's diet should include about 20 to 30 percent of calories from fat. Though the total number of grams you consume will depend on your caloric intake, you should never go below 20 grams of fat per day. You should try to avoid saturated fats from foods such as butter, lard, egg yolks, and red meat, as well as whole-fat dairy products.

Carbohydrate Intake, Before and After Playing or Practicing

While you are exercising, you should consume about 25 to 50 grams of carbohydrates and about 100 to 200 calories per hour to maintain your energy level. For example, a 16-ounce sports drink typically contains 28 grams of carbohydrates and 100 calories, and an energy bar may contain about 45 grams of carbohydrates.

For refueling, you should try to consume 1 to 1.5 grams per kilogram of carbohydrates within the first 30 minutes, and approximately 100 grams per hour for two to four hours after you finish exercising. For example, a 150-pound (68.2-kilogram) athlete should consume between 68 and 102 grams of carbohydrates within 30 minutes.

Here is the carbohydrate content, in grams, of some common foods:

- Bagel: 58
- Baked potato: 50
- Soft pretzel: 38
- Apple: 32
- Banana: 27
- Oatmeal: 27
- Bread (one slice): 11

Sports Drinks

Sports drinks are usually necessary only if you are going to be involved in an activity lasting more than 90 minutes. The best choices are those which contain a five percent carbohydrate solution. To get the carbohydrate content of a product, take the total grams of carbohydrates and divide by the total calories per serving.

Products containing high-fructose corn syrup can cause cramping, and should be avoided.

DEVELOPING A PREMATCH OR PREPRACTICE ROUTINE

Many people head straight from the office or school to the tennis court or gym. Others work out early in the morning or late at night. Regardless of your schedule, eating too much or too little before a workout can leave you feeling weak or nauseous afterwards.

Eating a proper preworkout meal can help give you the maximum amount of energy while easing indigestion, cramps, and stomach pain.

What to Eat

The best preworkout meals are balanced, including carbohydrates, protein, and a small amount of fat. You want to make sure your meal has been digested before you begin working out.

Greasy, fried foods that are heavy in fat take a long time to digest and can cause nausea if eaten before a workout. A good example of a preworkout meal is a turkey sandwich, a side salad, and a piece of fruit. The turkey sandwich has protein and carbohydrates, the salad has minerals and roughage to help you digest, and the fruit provides sugar and carbohydrate for added energy. Keep yourself hydrated by accompanying your preworkout meal with eight to 24 ounces of caffeine-free liquid.

A meal like this takes between three to four hours to digest, and is perfect if you are planning a workout that lasts about an hour or less.

If you are going to be working out for over an hour at a high level of intensity, treat your preworkout meal just like professional athletes treat their pregame meals. A preworkout meal usually consists of about one to four grams of carbohydrate for every kilogram of body weight. For longer and more intense workouts, you should eat closer to four grams of carbohydrate per kilogram (divide your weight in pounds by 2.2 to determine your weight in kilograms).

You should prepare yourself for a long workout by drinking plenty of fluids throughout the day. During a long match, drink 25 to 50 grams of carbohydrates every hour. Many premixed sports drinks make digesting carbohydrates easier.

When to Eat

To ensure proper digestion, it makes sense to eat three to four hours before your match or workout. If you were scheduled to play at 5:00 P.M., eating lunch at one o'clock would be right on target. You would be able to digest your food, avoid stomachaches, and have the optimal amount of sugars available for energy. If you eat lunch at noon, you might consider eating a carbohydrate snack right before you play to provide extra energy.

A Last-Second Boost

In general, everyone should drink eight to 24 ounces of fluid about an hour before a workout. If you have not had a meal in the last four hours prior to a workout, eating a piece of fruit or some crackers or drinking eight ounces of 100 percent fruit juice can help give you the extra energy you need to push yourself through an effective workout. Depending on the sensitivity of your stomach, you should eat your carbohydrate snack about an hour before a workout.

Some professional athletes use carbohydrate-and-protein supplements that are mixed with liquid for rapid absorption into the muscles. Eating a bagel or muffin right before a workout causes blood flow to go to the stomach rather than to the muscles for performance.

Postmatch Meal

You will burn more calories and deplete your store of glycogen the longer you work out. Athletes should replenish their glycogen stores within 30 minutes of ending a workout by consuming 1 to 1.5 grams of carbohydrate per kilogram of body weight. The average exerciser will not seriously deplete stored glycogen, but it is a good habit to practice carbohydrate refueling after exercise.

Many athletes may feel extra hunger after a workout and end up overeating. Some fruit juice or a carbohydrate snack immediately after a workout can ease this common urge.

Although your carbohydrate intake before you exercise can be important, it is more important to have a balanced, sensible diet that you follow week in and week out. A proper preworkout meal one day, followed by a week of fatty food, will almost certainly ensure you will not be performing at your peak.

18
GAMES

Learning to play tennis should not consist solely of hitting thousands of groundstrokes, volleys, and serves. It should incorporate different types of exercises and games that force players to develop different types of strokes, and, more important, to think on their feet and react quickly, particularly when they are fatigued. These skills can come in handy in the later stages of a tight match.

Following are some games that can be played using two to eight or more players.

Twenty-one

This game encourages players to rush the net, but also teaches them to do so when it is appropriate.

Begin with one player serving. For each winning shot from the baseline—one that the opponent cannot get to, instead of an unforced error by either player—the player scores one point. For every winning volley shot from the net, the player scores two points. The first player to reach 21 points wins.

Top of the Hill

Several players can play this game, with the number of players determining the number of courts used. Two players play on each court, one on each side, and each half of each court is given a number. For instance, if there are six players playing on three courts, the highest-ranked court—sides 1 and 2—is called the "top of the hill."

The player on the higher-ranked side serves to the player on the lower-ranked side, and one volley is played out. The winner of the rally moves on to the next court, except at the top of the hill, where the winner remains. The loser stays where she is and serves the next point on the same court. For example: the winner on the 5-6 court moves to the 3-4 court to play the loser of the previous point on that court. The winner on the 3-4 court moves to the 1-2 court to play the winner of the previous point on that court—the player at the top of the hill. The loser on the 1-2 court moves to the 5-6 court to play the loser of the previous point on that court.

The only place where the winner gets a point is at the top of the hill. The player who has collected the most points from the top of the hill at the end of a designated time is the winner.

Top of the Hill—Doubles

Top of the Hill changes slightly when it is played with doubles teams. Instead of winning one point, the players must win an entire game, unless the game at the top of the hill is over first. If so, all other games end and the team that is ahead is considered the winner. If a game is tied, one more point may be played. The players who have won the most games at the end of the designated time is the winner.

The player rotation is slightly different as well. As before, the top-of-the-hill winners stay on the same court and the losers go down to the lowest-ranked court; this time, however, they split up the team, with the players taking opposite sides of the net. The winners and losers of the other games also split up, unless they are about to enter the top-of-the-hill court. Otherwise, rotation remains the same.

Short Court

This game is good for developing quick reflexes, and it forces players to use touch and placement. It is just like regular tennis, except that the court is reduced to only the service courts. With one player on each side, play begins with a drop-ball serve (not an overhead serve). Each time the ball crosses the net, it must bounce in the service court. Players cannot hit the ball out of the air, or it will count as a point against them. Players also lose a point if the ball they hit does not land in the service court. Otherwise, scoring is the same as in regular tennis.

One on You

This game is a good one for playing at the beginning of a season, when players may be rusty and good rallies can be hard to come by.

To start with, each player gets three serves instead of two. This will promote more rallies by decreasing the number of double-faults. Once rallying begins, the scoring gets a little complicated, though players will soon get the hang of it. Basically, winners and forced errors are counted as normal, but an unforced error does not count as a full point; instead, a player must commit three unforced errors in a row to lose a point.

For example, if one player makes an unforced error on the first point, it is called "one on me." The second unforced error is "two on me." If a third unforced error is made, the opponent wins the point and leads, 15-love. If, however, a player has two unforced errors on her and the opponent makes an unforced error, the first players' errors are erased and the other player now has "one on her."

If a player hits a winner, all of the "on you" points are erased, and the player is awarded the point immediately.

Alley Rally

This is one of the best control games in tennis, and one of the most difficult. The rules and scoring are exactly the same as in regular tennis, but the playing area is limited to the alley only. Unlike "One on You," the points in this game rarely will come from winning shots, but instead will be errors when players' shots go outside the four-foot-wide alley area.

Horse

Like the basketball game of the same name, "Horse" teaches players to develop a wide variety of shots, and puts them on the spot when they have to imitate an opponent's shot. It also can provide some comic relief.

The first player announces a shot. It can be something simple, like a slice serve into the service court, or it can be something crazy, like hitting a lob shot into the backcourt while the player is on her knees. If the player misses the shot, the next player is free to create a new shot. But if the player successfully completes the shot she describes, the next player must duplicate the shot. If the second player is able to do so, the first player (or the third player if there are more than two) must do the shot again. This goes on until someone misses. That person has an "H." Play continues until someone has spelled out H-O-R-S-E, and loses the game.

Vic-O-Rama

Eight or more players can play this game. Players should divide into two teams, with one player from each team going out on the court to play the first point. After the point, the winner stays on, and one more member of her team joins her. The loser leaves the court, and the next player on her team takes her place, so that now two members of the first team are playing against one member of the second team.

If the first team wins again, it adds a third member of its team to the court, making it three against one. However, if the player from the second team wins, she adds another member of her team to the court while the three players from the first team leave the court and are replaced by one player from their team.

The team with the single player on the court gets to use the full court, while the other team—no matter how many of its players are on the court—must use the singles court. The game ends when one team has managed to win enough points in a row so that the entire team is on the court at once.

Handball Tennis

When players find themselves on a court without a racket, this is the perfect alternative. The game is the same as tennis, except only a small area of the court is used—usually the service courts—and hands are the main piece of equipment.

Players bat the ball back and forth with their hands. The hands must remain stiff, as catching the ball will cause a player to lose a point. Players are allowed to use both hands, though not at the same time.

Goalie

Mark off one section of a backboard or wall as the goal. One player stands in front of the goal area with her racket and does her best to keep the ball from going into the goal. The "shooter" tries to serve the ball past the goalie, who tries to block it with a volley. If she succeeds, the shooter must fire a shot with either a backhand or forehand. If more than one person is shooting, the players can take turns. Players switch with the goalie after a specified amount of time. The player with the most goals wins.

To keep the shooters far enough back to avoid injuring the goalie, draw a boundary line at least 10 feet back from the wall or backboard.

15-30-40-Game

To play 15-30-40-Game, players must first set up four targets on the backboard or wall. One should be marked 15, the next 30, the next 40, and the last GAME. One player serves to the wall. The next player gets the rebound and hits it toward the 15 target. If she gets it, that is her score and she moves on to 30; if she misses, the first player gets the rebound and tries for the 15 target. The rally ends when either player misses any of the targets, or if one player hits all four targets in order. The first player to do this wins the game. There are no deuce or ad points, and the winner is the one who gets two out of three sets, just as in regular tennis.

If the rally dies before someone wins the game, the player who made the bad shot is the one who serves to the wall. You cannot score on a serve.

Tennis Hockey

This is a variation of Goalie that can be played with groups of six or more players. Two goals should be marked off at both ends of the gym, the way it would be in regular hockey. Players divide into two teams, and two players are chosen goalies for their respective teams. As in Goalie, these players will have a lot of volleying work as they protect the goal.

The rest of the players take their positions on the floor. One team starts the play with a serve. Each team tries to get the ball into the opposite goal. Players may stop a ball flying past them by holding out their hand, but they may not catch the ball. Once the ball drops in front of them, they then hit it with their racket either to pass to a teammate or shoot for the goal. The team with the most goals at the end of a specified time period wins.

If play gets too rough with players wildly swinging their rackets, it is a good idea to give players their own square in the floor. They are not allowed out of the square, and they are responsible for any balls that come into it.

Tennis Volleyball

The rules in this game are similar to volleyball, although it is played on a tennis court. The net represents the volleyball net. The players divide into two equal teams, with at least three players on each team. Play begins with a tennis serve, and the ball should go to the person standing in the appropriate service court. The receiving team has three tries to get the ball back over the net without letting it hit the ground, even on the serve.

Play continues in this manner until the ball hits the ground or goes out of bounds. If the serving team is the winner, it gets a point. If the receiving team was the winner, it gets the serve. Points can only be won by the team that is serving.

Players can vary the rules, such as outlawing smashes and requiring that all shots be lofted first, to make rallies last longer.

Rotation Tennis

Players take up positions around the perimeter of the court (all four sides), and should be as evenly spaced as possible. Eight or more players can play, with each player playing for herself. The player nearest the center line on the baseline starts play by serving to the player nearest the center line on the other side of the court. After serving, she rotates clockwise, and the player to her right rotates into position on the baseline. The same rotation occurs on the other side of the court.

The object is then to keep the ball in play. If a player fails to do this, she is eliminated and must step outside the rotation. As more and more players get eliminated, it becomes increasingly difficult to get into position on time. Players find themselves sprinting around the court.

When there are three players remaining, a player's best bet is a lob shot, which will give her time to reach the other end of the court for the return shot. When two players remain, they play out the point to decide the eventual winner.

Target

Target is a game for two people, but many pairs can play it at once on the same court. It is a good game for practicing racket control.

Each pair of players should have three tennis balls. Two of the balls are placed opposite one another on the crosscourt alley lines. One player stands behind each one of these balls, and the third ball is the one used in play.

The game begins with a drop-hit. Players try to hit their opponent's target ball with the ball in play, but all hits must be little taps that the opponent can return. In other words, a player cannot smash the ball toward the target ball. The first player to hit the opponent's ball is the winner.

Canadian Doubles

What do you do when you want to play doubles and three players show up? A fun solution is Canadian doubles, which is played with three players.

One player is the singles player, and the other two are doubles players. The doubles' players side of the court includes the alleys, while the singles player's side uses just the singles court. The game is played like regular tennis, except the play must go to three sets, and each player must play an entire set as the singles player. At the end, the individual games are added up, and the player who has won the most games is the winner.

GLOSSARY

ace A serve that your opponent cannot reach before it hits the ground a second time.

advantage (or 'ad') The score one point after deuce. If you win the deuce point, it is your advantage, or your *ad*. If you win the next point, you win the game.

ad court The side of the court that the server serves to when the game score is advantage to the server or advantage to the returner; the same side (left-to-right) used for the second, fourth, and sixth points of the game.

alley The part of a tennis court between the singles sidelines and the doubles sidelines; also called the doubles alley.

approach shot A shot you hit just before you come to the net for a volley. An approach shot is usually played deep into your opponent's court or into the corner, which increases your chances of being able to volley her return for a winner.

Australian doubles A doubles positioning in which the net player on the serving team lines up on the same side as the server. This disguises the serving team's intentions and enables them to easily poach the service return.

backcourt The area from just behind the service line to behind the baseline.

backhand One of the basic strokes of tennis, named for the way in which the back of your hand faces the net as you hit the ball. A stroke played from the left side of the body for a right-handed player or the right side of the body for a left-handed player.

baseline The line at each end of the court that runs parallel to the net and marks the lengthwise boundary of the court.

baseline rally A series of shots between two players who stay on or behind the baseline.

best-of-three sets The standard length of matches at the high school and collegiate level. The first player to win two sets wins the match.

block A short stroke that is used to return a fast shot like a serve.

Both-Up, Both-Back   Offensive and defensive positioning in doubles. In Both-Up, both players are at the net and attacking, while in Both-Back, both players are at the baseline, usually when both opponents are at the net.

break   When the returning player wins a game on her opponent's serve.

break point   When the returning player needs one point to win her opponent's service game. Break points are some of the most crucial points in many match.

center line   The line that runs perpendicular from the middle of the net and splits the forecourt into the two service courts.

center mark   A four-inch line that runs perpendicular to the baseline and divides the baseline in half. The server must stand on either side of the center mark when serving.

change of ends (changeover)   The players switch ends of the court after every odd-numbered game, beginning with the first game of the match.

chip and charge   A strategy in which a player will hit a low, backspin slice shot (chip) and approach the net (charge) to try and volley her opponent's return.

chop   Another word for slice: a shot hit with a downward motion to produce backspin. Used to take the pace off a fast incoming shot, or to hit a drop shot.

closed face   When the angle of the racket is pointing at less than 90 degrees, usually when hitting a topspin shot.

Continental grip   A common way of holding the racket to hit volleys, serve, or hit slice shots from the forehand or backhand side (see Chapter 4, Grips).

crosscourt   A shot played diagonally across the court; for example, from the right corner of your side of the court to the right corner of your opponent's side of the court.

deuce   When the score reaches 40-40 in a game. To win a game that has reached deuce, a player must win the game by two points.

deuce court   The side of the court that the server serves to when the game score is deuce; the same side (right-to-left) used for the first, third, and fifth points of the game.

dink   A shot that is hit just over the net, usually at an angle, to lure your opponent to the net so that you can hit a lob or passing shot.

double-fault   When the server hits consecutive serves that do not land in the returner's service court, whether by landing outside the boundaries of the service court or by hitting the net. The returner wins the point when the server double-faults.

down the line   A shot that goes parallel to the sidelines; for example, from your forehand to your opponent's backhand, if you are both right-handed.

drive shot A strong, straight shot hit with little topspin or back-spin; commonly used as a passing shot when your opponent is at the net.

drop shot A short shot hit with exaggerated backspin that just clears the net and dies there. Can be an outright winner, or it can set up a high return by your opponent that can be volleyed for a winner.

drop volley A volley on which you take pace off your opponent's shot and drop the ball just over the net and out of reach of your opponent.

Eastern grip A common way of holding the racket that produces top-spin on forehands or backhands; also, a common grip used for serving with spins and slices.

fault A serve that does not land inside your opponent's service court, either by landing outside the box's boundaries or by hitting the net.

flat shot A shot hit without topspin or backspin. A flat shot will have more pace (speed), and will bounce lower than a shot with top-spin and higher than a shot with backspin.

follow-through The finish of any stroke, and a key component that is often overlooked. Your follow-through will dictate the direction, pace, and length of the shot.

foot fault When a player steps on or over the baseline before making contact with the ball while serving. The result is the same as if the serve had been a fault.

forecourt The area of the court between the service lines and the net.

forehand One of the basic strokes in tennis, and one that is most players' strongest shot. It is played from the right side of the body for a right-handed player, and the left side of the body for a left-handed player.

game scoring A tennis game consists of a minimum of four points— 15, 30, 40, and game—and a maximum of infinity. The first player to win game point wins the game, but she has to win by at least two points. The score is normally called by the serving player, with the serving player's score recited first. For example, if the server won the first point but the returner won the next two points, the score would be "15-30."

game point When a player is one point from winning the game. When either the server or returner has reached 40 and is ahead by at least one point; or, when the players have reached deuce, one player has won the next point, and is one point from winning the game.

grip The way in which you hold the racket, which affects the kind of shots you are able to hit. Also, a term to describe the synthetic material that covers the handle of your racket to prevent it from slipping out of your hand.

groundstroke   Any shot on the forehand or backhand side that is played after the ball has bounced. Groundstrokes are referred to by many players as "groundies."

half (mid-) court   The area of the court around the service line.

half-volley   A half-groundstroke, half-volley, which means a shot that is played on a short hop, immediately after the ball has bounced and when it is on its upward rise.

hard court   An all-weather court surface, usually asphalt or concrete or a mixture of the two. Can play faster or slower depending on the mix used in the surface.

The Hole   The diagonal gap between the net player and the baseline player in doubles which must be covered when the opposing net player is playing the ball.

kick serve   A serve hit with exaggerated spin so that it bounces up and away from the returner. This is an effective second serve.

let   An interruption of play, caused by a ball rolling onto the court or anything else that may distract the players. When a let is called, the point is replayed. Also, a let is called on a serve if the serve touches the net and lands in the service court. In this case, the serve is replayed.

line judge/linesperson   The official who is responsible for determining if a ball has landed inside or outside the boundaries of the court.

lob   A shot that arches high into the air and usually lands in the backcourt. Can be used as an offensive weapon if an opponent has come to the net, or a defensive ploy if you are trapped in the backcourt.

love   A score of zero. When you are serving and your opponent wins the first point, the score is "love-15."

lucky loser   A player who has lost in the qualifying event before the main tournament, but is able to get into the main draw because another player has defaulted or been injured.

match   Consists of a best-of-three or best-of-five sets format, or any other agreed-on format.

match point   When a player is one point away from winning the match.

mini-break   When the server loses a point, or two points, during a tiebreak.

net   A call sometimes substituted for let when a serve hits the net and drops into the service court, and is therefore replayed.

no-man's land   The area between the service line and the baseline. It has this name because straying in there can be risky: you will end up hitting difficult, in-between shots like half-volleys or low volleys because you will be too far up to hit a regular groundstroke and too far back to hit a regular volley.

nonhitting hand Your left hand if you are right-handed, and vice versa. Proper positioning and movement of the nonhitting hand is crucial to maintaining balance and fluidity during your strokes.

One-Up, One-Back Standard doubles positioning in which one player plays at net and the other at the baseline.

open face When the angle of the racket is pointing at greater than 90 degrees, usually when hitting a backspin shot.

open stance A hitting position for forehands and backhands in which your feet are nearly parallel and your body starts and finishes facing the net.

overhead Also called a smash. A shot hit over the head, using the same motion used for a serve. A too-short lob will usually result in an overhead.

overrule When the chair umpire changes a line call made by a linesperson.

passing shot A shot made when your opponent is at the net that she cannot reach.

poach In doubles, a lateral move by the net player to cut off a shot by an opponent before it reaches the backcourt.

point penalty A penalty that is assessed by the chair umpire when a player is guilty of using foul language, abusing the ball or a racket, or other code violations.

pro set A modified scoring system in which the first player or doubles team to reach eight games wins the match.

qualifying tournament (qualies) A competition held in the days leading up to a tournament that allows lower-ranked players the opportunity to gain entry into the main tournament.

rally Any series of shots that occurs after the serve.

ready position The stance used when you are awaiting your opponent's return.

receiver The player who is receiving serve from the server.

return Usually refers to the stroke used to return a serve, but can be used to describe any shot during a rally.

second serve The server is allowed two serves on each point, providing there are no let serves that touch the net and land in the service court. If the first serve is a fault, the server is allowed to take a second serve. A strong, consistent second serve is a crucial part of any player's game.

seeding Ranking of players for a tournament, with the purpose of keeping "seeded" players—the top players, basically—from playing each other until the later rounds.

Semi-Western grip A less common way of holding the racket that allows you to hit the ball with exaggerated topspin. In the Semi-

Western grip, the hand is positioned between an Eastern grip and a full Western grip.

serve and volley   A style of play in which the server approaches the net behind her serve to put pressure on her opponent and force a weak or erratic return that can be volleyed for a winner.

serve/service   The start to every point is the serve. The first serve of each game is made from the right-hand side of the server's court diagonally to the opposite service court. The next point is served from the left side of the server's court diagonally to the other service court. The server alternates sides on each point, and must keep her feet to the right or left of the center mark in the middle of the baseline. The server gets two serves on each point, unless there is a let, in which case the serve is replayed.

service line   The line that runs parallel to the net and serves as the back boundary of the service court. The distance from the service line to the net is 21 feet.

service court   The two halves of the forecourt that the ball must be served into to start each point. The service courts measure 21 feet front to back and 13 1/2 feet side to side.

set   A set consists of a minimum of six games. To win a set, a player must win six games, plus win at least two more games than her opponent. If players are tied at six games apiece, a 12-point tiebreak set is played to decide the winner of the set.

set point   When one player is within one point of winning the set.

sidelines   The side boundaries of the court: 27 feet across for singles, 36 feet across for doubles.

slice (underspin)   A shot that is usually hit with a downward motion that creates backspin, or slice, which keeps the ball low and creates a low bounce on your opponent's side of the court, forcing her to hit up on the ball.

slice serve   A serve hit with a three-quarters motion that puts side spin on the ball, making it difficult for your opponent to hit a clean return. Can be used effectively as a second serve.

smash   See Overhead.

spin serve   Any type of serve that puts spin on the ball in an attempt to create a high or erratic bounce that can throw off your opponent's timing and cause a weak return.

split step   The movement you make between getting in the ready position and hitting the ball. You hop slightly and split your feet apart about three or four inches wider than when you started, timed to the moment your opponent's racket makes contact with the ball. This gets you ready to move quickly to the left or right.

The T   The juncture formed by the service line and the center line.

tiebreak   A 12-point miniset that determines the winner of a set in which the players are tied at 6-6. To win a tiebreak, one player must reach at least seven points with a two-point margin. Whichever player was due to serve the next game when the set score reaches 6-6 is the first server in the tiebreak. She serves the first point, after which the serves alternate two at a time for each player. The players change ends after every six points.

topspin   A shot caused by a low-to-high stroke motion, causing the ball to spin forward and dip after it crosses the net. Hitting with topspin can allow you to swing harder, because the spin forces the ball down and enables it to land in the court.

umpire (chair umpire)   The official who keeps score and has the power to overrule the linespersons on line calls. The umpire also has the power to assess penalties against players for abusive language, ball or racket abuse, or other code infractions.

unforced error   A mis-hit or an errant shot hit when you are not under pressure by your opponent (e.g., when your opponent is not at the net or has not forced you into a defensive position).

volley   Hitting the ball before it hits the ground. Most volleys are hit when you are close to the net.

Western grip   A less common way of holding the racket that produces exaggerated topspin on forehands and backhands. Many clay court specialists use the Western grip to put heavy topspin on their shots to counteract the slower court surface.

wide-body   The thickness of a racket's head. Today's head frames are nearly as twice as thick as the wooden rackets made in the 1960s and 1970s, and produce much more power as a result.

winner   A shot that your opponent can barely touch or is unable to reach (a "clean" winner).

wrong-foot   Hitting behind your opponent. For example, hitting a ball to your opponent's backhand, then hitting another ball to her backhand as she is attempting to move back into position, which puts her off-balance and unable to make a strong return.

TENNIS ORGANIZATIONS

ATP Tour
200 ATP Tour Boulevard
Ponte Vedra Beach, FL 32082
Telephone: (904) 285-8000
Fax: (904) 285-5966

The California Tennis Network
Telephone: (323) 259-4424
E-mail: pj@californiatennis.com

Intercollegiate Tennis Association
P.O. Box 71
Princeton University
Princeton, NJ 08544
Telephone: (609) 258-1686
Fax: (609) 258-2935
E-mail: ita@tennisonline.com

International Health, Racquet & Sportsclub Association
263 Summer Street
Boston, MA 02210
Telephone: (617) 951-0055
Fax: (617) 951-0056
E-mail: info@ihrsa.org

International Tennis Hall of Fame
Newport Casino
194 Bellevue Avenue
Newport, RI 02840
Telephone: (401) 849-3990
Fax: (401) 849-8780
E-mail: tennisfame@aol.com

International Tennis Federation
Palliser Road, Baron's Court
London W14 9EN, England
Telephone: 44-171-381-8060
Fax: 44-171-386-3989
E-mail: itf@itftennis.com

Maureen Connolly Brinker Foundation
P.O. Box 7065
Dallas, TX 75209
Telephone: (214) 352-7978
Fax: (214) 352-9708

National Association of Intercollegiate Athletics (NAIA)
6120 South Yale Avenue
Suite 1450
Tulsa, OK 74136
Telephone: (918) 494-8828
Fax: (918) 494-8841

National Federation of State High School Associations
P.O. Box 20626
Kansas City, MO 64195-0626
Telephone: (816) 464-5400
Fax: (816) 464-5571

National Foundation of Wheelchair Tennis
940 Calle Amanecer
Suite B
San Clemente, CA 92672
Telephone: (714) 361-3663
Fax: (714) 361-6822
E-mail: NFWT@aol.com

National Junior College Athletic Association (NJCAA)
P.O. Box 7305
Colorado Springs, CO 80933-7305
Telephone: (719) 590-9788
Fax: (719) 590-7324

National Collegiate Athletic Association (NCAA)
700 West Washington Street
P.O. Box 6222
Indianapolis, IN 46206-6222
Telephone: (317) 917-6222
Fax: (913) 917-6888

NCAA Initial-Eligibility Clearinghouse
2255 North Dubuque Road
P.O. Box 4044
Iowa City, IA 52243-4044
Telephone: (800) 638-3731

U.S. Professional Tennis Association
One USPTA Center
3535 Briarpark Drive
Houston, TX 77042
Telephone: (713) 97-USPTA (978-7782)
Fax: (713) 978-7780
E-mail: uspta@uspta.org

U.S. Professional Tennis Registry
P.O. Box 4739
Hilton Head, SC 29938
Telephone: (800) 421-6289
Fax: (803) 686-2033

U.S. Racquet Stringers Association
P.O. Box 40
Del Mar, CA 92014-9959
Telephone: (619) 481-3543
Fax: (619) 481-0624
E-mail: usrsa@aol.com

U.S. Tennis Association
National headquarters:
70 West Red Oak Lane
White Plains, NY 10604
Telephone: (914) 696-7000
Fax: (914) 696-7269
Regional offices:
Caribbean Tennis Association
P.O. Box 40439
Minillas Station
Santurce, Puerto Rico 00940
Telephone: (809) 724-7425
Fax: (809) 724-7990

Eastern Tennis Association
550 Mamaroneck Ave.
Suite 505
Harrison, NY 10528
Telephone: (914) 698-0414
Fax: (914) 698-2471

USTA/Florida Section
1280 S.W. 36th Avenue
Suite 305
Pompano Beach, FL 33069
Telephone: (954) 968-3434
Fax: (954) 968-3986

Hawaii Pacific Tennis Association
2615 South King Street
Suite 2A
Honolulu, HI 96826
Telephone: (808) 955-6696
Fax: (808) 955-8363

Intermountain Tennis Association
1201 South Parker Road
Suite 200
Denver, CO 80231
Telephone: (303) 695-4117
Fax: (303) 695-6518

USTA/Mid-Atlantic
2230 George C. Marshall Drive
Suite E
Falls Church, VA 22043
Telephone: (703) 560-9480
Fax: (703) 560-9505

USTA/Middle States
460 Glennie Circle
King of Prussia, PA 19406
Telephone: (610) 277-4040
Fax: (610) 239-8999

USTA Missouri Valley
801 Walnut Street
Suite 100
Kansas City, MO 64106
Telephone: (816) 472-6882
Fax: (816) 472-6677

USTA/New England
181 Wells Avenue
Newton Centre, MA 02159
Telephone: (617) 964-2030
Fax: (617) 244-8973

USTA/Northern California
1350 South Loop Road
Suite 100
Alameda, CA
Telephone: (510) 748-7373
Fax: (510) 748-7377

Northwestern Tennis Association
5525 Cedar Lake Road
St. Louis Park, MN 55416
Telephone: (612) 546-0709
Fax: (612) 546-7378

USTA/Pacific Northwest
4840 S.W. Western Avenue
Suite 300
Beaverton, OR 97005
Telephone: (503) 520-1877
Fax: (503) 520-0133

Southern Tennis Association
Spalding Woods Office Park
3850 Holcomb Bridge Road
Suite 305
Norcross, GA 30092
Telephone: (770) 368-8200
Fax: (770) 368-9091

Southern California Tennis Association/San Diego
P.O. Box 250015
Los Angeles, CA 90024
Telephone: (310) 208-3838
Fax: (310) 824-7691

USTA Southwest Section
6330-2 East Thomas Road
Suite 120
Scottsdale, AZ 85251
Telephone: (602) 947-9293
Fax: (602) 947-1102

Texas Tennis Association
2111 Dickson
Suite 33
Austin, TX 78704
Telephone: (512) 443-1334
Fax: (512) 443-4748

Western Tennis Association
8720 Castle Creek Parkway
Suite 329
Indianapolis, IN 46250
Telephone: (317) 577-5130
Fax: (317) 577-5131

U.S. Tennis Court & Track Builders Association
3525 Ellicott Mills Drive
Suite N
Ellicott City, MD 21043-4547
Telephone: (410) 418-4875
Fax: (410) 418-4805
E-mail: info@ustctba.com

WTA Tour
1266 East Main Street
4th Floor
Stamford, CT 06902-3546
Telephone: (203) 978-1740
Fax: (203) 978-1702

FURTHER READING

Frediani, Paul. *Net Flex: 10 Minutes a Day to Better Play.* New York: Hatherleigh Press, 2001.

Metzler, Michael. *Tennis: Mastering the Basics with the Personalized Sports Instruction System (A Workbook Approach).* San Francisco: Benjamin/Cummings, 2000.

Murray, John F., and Rick Frey. *Smart Tennis: How to Play and Win the Mental Game (Smart Sport Series).* New York: Jossey Bass, 1999.

Todd Ellenbecker. *Complete Conditioning for Tennis.* Champaign, Ill.: Human Kinetics Publishing, 1998.

United States Tennis Association. *Tennis Tactics: Winning Patterns of Play.* Champaign, Ill.: Human Kinetics Publishing, 1996.

Yandell, John. *Visual Tennis.* 2d ed. Champaign, Ill.: Human Kinetics Publishing, 1999.

INDEX